SC
M
LEGENDS

Malcolm Archibald

Chambers

CHAMBERS
An imprint of Larousse plc
43–45 Annandale Street
Edinburgh EH7 4AZ

First published by Chambers 1992
Reprinted 1994

A CIP catalogue record for this book is
available from the British Library

ISBN 0 550 20071 1

Illustrations by John Haxby and Janet MacKay
© Larousse plc
Cover design by John Marshall

Typeset by Buccleuch Printers Ltd, Hawick
Printed in Singapore by
Singapore National Printers Ltd

Contents

Introduction

To outsiders, Scotland has always seemed a place of mystery. Beyond the ramparts of Roman civilization, beyond the mailed grasp of Norman Europe, the northernmost nation of the so-called Celtic fringe, Scotland has often been viewed askance.

'This is the end of the habitable world' is symptomatic of the Roman – and not only the Roman – view of Scotland.

The inhabitants of Scotland encouraged this view of their separateness. The Culdee Church for example, centred on Iona, was never quite convinced that the religious practices ordered by the Roman Catholic Pope and observed by the remainder of Christianity superseded those of the few thousand monks of Alba. Iona still remains different: its tranquil atmosphere tends to bring a certain purity of thought to a materialistic world.

And Wallace, whose stature rises above common humanity to enter the very world of legend, thought the imperialistic aim of the first English Edward very similar to that of Agricola, although it was not until some years after his betrayal and judicial murder that his thoughts were enshrined in words. The Declaration of Arbroath of 1320 states the case finely:

> So long as 100 of us remain alive, we shall not, in any degree, be subject to the domination of the English. It is not for honour, glory nor riches that we fight and contend for, but liberty alone, which no honest man will lose but with his life.

There was freedom in Scotland. At the same time as England was fighting its serfs wars, serfdom was dying in Scotland. But there was also widespread poverty. While the men of Moray and Galloway were resisting the new feudalism of Norman knights, the 12th-century Arab geographer, Idrisi, described Scotland as desolate, without inhabitants, towns or villages. Thus, this freedom had to be paid for by the suffering of the Scots people and the resulting neglected and arid soil.

This poverty, and the willingness to repulse invasion, tended to dissuade travellers from visiting Scotland. Save for a few hardy souls and brave religious men, the visitor usually came bearing a sword and, with it, ill-will. Their recollection of the Scots, not surprisingly, was tainted. In their tales, carried from castle siege and shrouded camp-fire, Scotland was a grim, frightening place. Exiled Scots furthered the idea. Byron, 'Mad, bad and dangerous to know', termed Scotland a land of meanness, sophistry and mist. For meanness read insufficiency and for sophistry, subtlety. The mist is real.

Add to these half-truths the nature of the people, always ready with a story to help them survive the long nights of winter, and it is no wonder that Scotland is a place of legend.

The dictionary definition of a myth is 'an ancient traditional story of gods or heroes, offering an explanation of some fact or phenomenon . . . a commonly held belief that is untrue, or without foundation.' On the other hand, a legend is a traditional story.

With Scotland's intricate history, full of twists and dead ends, the lack of strong central government and the sheer individuality of the people, it is not surprising that there should be a vast amount of legendary material. Oral tradition was strong in the Highlands; the Borders and the north-east are ballad country. Viking and English invaders stole or destroyed a great deal of Scotland's documentary records. All this leads to folk-tales having a more than normal importance, in some cases taking the place of properly recorded history.

The myths and legends which follow have been chosen primarily because they illustrate the multi-faceted character of Scotland. There is no typical Scottish legend, just as there is no typical Scottish person, or typical Scottish scene. There cannot be such a legend, or person, or scene because of the variety of essentials which make up Scotland. One thing which most Scots have in common is individuality; dig beneath the veneer of 20th-century life and the basic Scot will glower through. He or she might be a Shetland Scot, with blood nearly pure Norse, or an Aberdonian Scot with the Pictish strain clearly seen, the Gael of the west or the Briton of Ayrshire; indeed he or she could be a combination of them all, an alloy like Scotland herself.

This is equally true of the legends: each portrays an idea, or a region, or a dream which is important to the understanding of the nation of the Scots.

Significantly there was never a king of Scotland, but a king of Scots. The king was a leader of people, for it was the people who mattered, however dear they held the land. The 'Community of the Realm' mattered as much as the realm itself, for the community was the realm. This collection of myths and legends aims to illustrate the depth of history, diversity of culture and range of habitat of the Scot.

Symbolic Scotland

It takes much to embody the character of a nation, and Scotland, in common with other countries, has many symbols which are recognizable as unique to herself.

The Flag

The first and possibly most obvious symbol of any nation is its flag, and Scotland has two, each with a distinctive story and a part in shaping the nation.

Some time in the latter half of the eighth century when national boundaries within the islands of Britain were still fluctuating, there was war between the Picts of Alba and the Angles of Northumbria. At this time Alba was mainly north of the Forth, Northumbria stretched from the Humber to north of the Tweed while somewhere in between lay a nebulous border. An army of Northumbrians, led by Athelstan, marched north, through the fertile lands of Lothian, while a Pictish army under one Hungus or Angus tramped south to meet them . . .

Not far from the fort of Dunpender – Traprain Law – the two armies met each other and camped for the night, anticipating a conclusive battle the next day. Already these people were enemies, the Picts having repulsed a Northumbrian attempt at conquest in 685, so each knew the other's capabilities and respected their opponent's strength.

On that tense night before the imminent battle, there might have been a breeze from the sea, whispering through the grass in mocking mimicry of wounded men, and stars might have glinted above the dim outline of Lammermuir. One man, the Pictish king, Hungus, had no trouble sleeping however, and he dreamed vividly.

Saint Andrew, whose bones had recently been received in Kilrymont, Fife (now St Andrews), appeared to the Pictish king. In the dream, the fisherman promised victory to the Picts. Hungus

1

woke before dawn, spread the word round his army and the hillmen and plainsmen of Alba grasped at the hope given as they tested sword and spear.

To ride to battle and fight on foot was the Alban way. The army would pace toward the enemy, their hands tight on spearshafts, their eyes warily counting the Angle hordes. And in the sky above, gleaming white against the deep blue, the Saltire cross of Andrew proved the worth of the word of a saint. Emboldened, the Picts roared their battle-cry and set on the Angles.

Tradition tells of a great victory, with Athelstan killed and his army scattered. From that day the Picts took the Saltire as their national flag; in time the emblem passed on to the united Scottish-Pictish kingdom. This makes the Saltire the oldest national flag in the world.

To this day the Saltire flies above the village of Athelstaneford in East Lothian, cared for by the Kirk. The story is enshrined beneath the standard.

If the Saltire became the flag of the Scots, the Lion Rampant is the royal standard of Scotland. It was King William I (1143–1214) who sported the roaring red lion as his heraldic device, thus earning himself the sobriquet 'William the Lion'. (Although another legend has him as William, 'Lion of Justice'.) It is possible that the lion had been symbolic of Scotland centuries before.

Charlemagne is reputed to have let the contemporary Scottish king use French lilies as 'a defence to the lion of Scotland'. This was proof of an alliance between the two nations. This alliance was based on a mutual fear of English aggression, and was bonded by a company of Scots soldiers who acted as Charlemagne's bodyguard.

Perhaps the Lion Rampant made King William look like a warrior, but his actions were too impetuous to make him a good king. After a victorious campaign which regained Caithness for Scotland, William thrust down into England. Emerging from a Northumbrian mist, William came across a group of knights, believed they were his own and rode towards them. When he discovered the knights were English, he couched lance and charged – only to be captured. His ransom cost Scotland dear: William paid homage to the English king for the realm of Scotland and this act of submission encouraged Edward I of England (1239–1307) in his later claim for the Scottish crown.

Interestingly, the same lion which had charged rampant on William's shield reared in stubborn defiance to reveal the rebirth of nationhood within Scotland. When Stirling Castle was under siege in 1304, Edward Longshanks of England had his army arrayed beneath the walls and the Scots garrison was trapped within. There was no hope of relief; the armies of independence were scattered, English knights held all strongholds between Inverness and the Cheviot Hills and only a few handfuls of brave men sheltered in the forests to fight the invader. By the rules of chivalry Sir William Oliphant, the Perthshire knight who defended Stirling, was in rebellion, but when Longshanks demanded of whom he held the castle, Oliphant pointed to the fluttering flag. 'Of the Lion,' he said. The Lion Rampant: symbol of Scotland.

The Thistle

As a personification of the prickly Scottish temperament, the thistle could not have been better chosen. Once again it is necessary to delve deep into the past to find out why this plant was selected, and once again the answer comes from a time of

3

conflict and national peril. This time the Vikings were the aggressors: an enemy which Hollywood has made appear a laughing band of romantic freebooters; however the reality was very different. From 795 Scotland was under assault by a wave of these vicious men who descended on undefended home-steads and plundered the delicate civilization built up by generations of Christian monks. Centuries later the Norse were Christianized, but the attacks continued. Not until 1266 were the Western Isles returned to Scottish rule.

Caught off guard, Scotland reeled beneath the shock of invasion, before defending herself with a vigour which checked the Norse attack. During the reign of Kenneth III (997–1005), a fleet of longships slid into the east coast and the crews crept on to land. There was a Scottish camp on top of a hill and a dark night to conceal attack. The Vikings crept stealthily up the grassy slope, barefoot to ensure silence, their swords and shields held carefully.

In Scotland, however, even the land helps repel invaders and one of the Norsemen stood on a thistle. His yell was heard by a sentry, the camp was roused and the Vikings repelled. King Kenneth was so grateful to the thistle that he adopted it as the national emblem.

Another version of this legend attributes the legendary King Achius with the appropriation of the thistle. This king is said to have founded the Order of the Thistle in the ninth century, limiting the number of knights to 13, including himself. Unfortunately, this story has yet to be proved, but there definitely is an Order of the Knights of the Thistle which commenced – or was refounded – by James VII in 1687. The Order has had a chequered history but today is firmly anchored in St Giles Cathedral, Edinburgh.

The Knights have the motto 'Nemo me impune lacessit', which translates as 'No one assails me with impunity', but is more commonly read as 'Wha daur meddle wi' me'. This motto is also used by Scotland as a nation and, thinking of the spiny prickles of the thistle, could hardly be bettered.

Tartan

Much has been written about tartan and there are perhaps more myths believed about this complex pattern of checks than about any other part of Scottish tradition. Nothing is more symbolic of Scottish dress than tartan; to the outsider, tartan is Scotland, whether covering a rush of fighting clansmen in historic times or flashed in gaudy showmanship by raucous football supporters at Hampden Park. By and large, this is a true, if distorted, belief. The ancient Celts, one or two branches of whom helped found the Scottish nation, wore a forerunner of tartan. They wore great cloaks decorated with bright checks and stripes, a taste for colour which has remained with the Celtic peoples to this day.

By the 13th century the Highland Gaels had the name 'breacan' for tartan, and within 300 years King James V (1512–42) was buying ells (ell=varying measures of cloth) of 'Heland tartane'. Different areas of the Highlands had different patterns of breacan, possibly depending as much on the availability of natural dyes as on the intentional design of the weaver. However, there were no formally set tartans for individual clans until well after the destruction of the clan system in the years following the 1745 rising. A study of pre-1746 portraits will reveal individuals wearing more than one tartan, few, if any, of which conform to the generally recognized setts (set(t) =pattern of tartan) of today.

5

In 1747 the wearing of tartan was banned by law to all except the military, a measure which continued until 1782, but the tartans which re-emerged thereafter were imperfect copies of the original. However, the very fact of proscription proves that tartan was seen as a form of national – or at least Highland – dress at the time of the 1745. Tartan became popular after the visit of King George IV to Holyrood in 1822, although the names applied to the various setts have nothing to do with the clans of earlier centuries.

It was Queen Victoria and her German husband Albert who finally gave the seal of approval to the once despised breacan, and their tartan-bedecked palace at Balmoral remains a monument to the queen's passion for Scotland.

For a while there was an industry in manufacturing and naming bright tartans: one being sold to a plantation owner in the West Indies for the purpose of clothing his slaves; the vivid colouring making any escapee easier to identify. Today's tartans then – and the list continues to grow – are not the same as were worn before the 1745, but their origin is undoubtedly ancient and plainly Scottish. And who is to say that the tartan sported in 1745 was the same as in 1545? Change is natural to humanity and the tartans of today can be considered as Scottish as they ever were.

The Bagpipes

Tartan may be a Scottish visual legend, but the Highland bagpipes are renowned as the most distinctively audible representation of Scotland. As seems to have been a frequent occurrence in Scottish history, this is an example of a once-widespread practice becoming localized. The bagpipes did not originate in Scotland; as an Indo-European instrument their use ranges from Pakistan to Ireland, but it was the pipers of the Scottish Highlands who gained international fame.

Bagpipes are known as 'pipes of war' and in recent years this has been proved correct. Through the last three centuries at least, the image of kilted pipers leading advancing soldiers to battle has become branded into folklore and expectations. Waterloo

and the stubborn redcoated squares of Highlanders faced cannonade and cavalry with the pipes skirling behind them. Dargai Heights and a wounded piper urged the Gordon Highlanders against waiting Afghan warriors. Loos and the defiant wail of Laidlaw's pipes sounded amidst drifting clouds of German gas in 1915. El Alamein and the 51st Division marching their bayonets against the Afrika Korps in 1942.

Yet the ancient Gael used the Carnyx, a huge war trumpet, to encourage them to battle, and the harp, strummed by iron-fingered bards, was the musical instrument to relax with. Nevertheless the bagpipes were important too and have become synonymous with Scotland and do, in fact, figure in many legends and stories.

Of all the Scottish pipers the most famous – and arguably the most skilled – were the MacCrimmons of Boreraig in Skye. Hundreds of years ago, Ian Og MacCrimmon was playing in Slochd nam Piobarean, the Piper's Hollow, when a fairy queen appeared. So impressed was the fairy by MacCrimmon's music that she gave him a silver chanter which played the sweetest music he had ever heard.

Of course MacCrimmon and the fairy fell in love

and from that day on the MacCrimmons were the best pipers in the world. They were certainly the hereditary pipers to MacLeod of Dunvegan and their piping school was renowned.

Another legend tells of the Black Lad Mac-Crimmon, who was denied the chance to play the pipes by his father. One day when his father was out, the lad took the chanter and was playing it when a fairy appeared and asked if he would prefer success without skill or skill with no success. The Black Lad chose the latter, so the fairy plucked out one of her own hairs, wound it round the chanter and helped the boy play a tune. From then on the Black Lad was the finest piper in the world.

In reality Donald Mor and Patrick Og MacCrimmon altered the pattern of the piobaireachd (the 'classical' form of bagpipe music) to make it more flexible, adding to its already considerable beauty. And for a fitting memorial to a school of piping whose like will probably never be seen again, here is the third verse of *'Cha till MacCruimean'* (No more, MacCrimmon) – the departure of the 4th Camerons . . .

And there in front of the men who were
    marching,
With feet that made no mark,
The grey old ghosts of the ancient fighters
Come back again from the dark;
And in front of them all MacCrimmon piping
A weary tune and sore:
On the gathering day, for ever and ever,
MacCrimmon comes no more.

(Ewart Alan Mackintosh)

The MacCrimmons' claim, however, could be challenged by the MacArthurs, one branch of whom piped for MacDonald of Sleat, another for the Islay MacDonalds. Perhaps a piping competition would have been an idea as a change from the never-ending butchery of clan warfare?

Jacobite Legends

The name of Bonnie Prince Charlie has come down the centuries to epitomize the tragic romance of Scotland. There are perhaps more books and legends concerning the bonnie prince than any other Scottish personality. He is seen as the man who led the last Scottish rising against the English (which is completely false), as the last representative of the ancient Scottish line of kings (which is slightly more correct), as a tartan-bedecked hero (which is questionable), and as a hardy adventurer protected by brave and loyal Highlanders (which is undeniably true).

Charles Edward Stuart (1720–88) was the grandson of James VII, who had been deposed from the throne of Scotland and England in 1688 owing to his intolerant Catholicism. William of Orange and Mary, James's daughter, became joint monarchs, and for the next half-century the Stuarts attempted to regain the throne which many believed was rightfully theirs.

The first Jacobite attempt was made in 1689, when John Graham of Claverhouse, Viscount Dundee (c.1649–89), gathered the pro-Jacobite clans and led them south. Claverhouse was already a figure of legend in Scotland, known as 'Bluidy Clavers' in the south because of his ferocious work in suppressing the Covenanters (Presbyterians who were persecuted by the Stuart kings). Claverhouse was reputed to have sold his soul to the devil, to be able to transform wine into clotted blood and to be invulnerable to ordinary bullets. Followers of King James VII thought otherwise: they termed him 'Bonnie Dundee' and expected great things of him.

To meet the gathering clans the government ordered Mackay of Scourie to lead a pro-William army north. Regular regiments were joined by Covenanters keen to revenge themselves on their oppressors. This was not a straight Highland–Lowland confrontation; among Mackay's redcoats were some Highlanders, including one Donald MacBean.

Mackay led his army through the pass of Killiecrankie and came across Dundee's Jacobites. Stationed as sentry on the pass was Donald MacBean. The battle was over quickly; Dundee's men charged, the redcoats broke and ran, the Highlanders followed and plundered the baggage. Unsupported at the head of the pass, MacBean was faced by a horde of broadsword-wielding Jacobites eager for blood. Not surprisingly, MacBean fled, but he could not run far; the gorge of Killiecrankie barred his escape, a deep rocky ravine with the River Garry roaring down below; MacBean was trapped.

Howling their battle slogans, the Jacobite clansmen poured towards MacBean; a glance back, a fearful look forwards and MacBean chanced the chasm. Twenty feet across but MacBean's adrenalin powered him over; the roar of a musket behind him, tearing pain in his shoulder as the musket ball hit, but MacBean was over. He survived the pursuit and often boasted of his exploit, showing the scar on his shoulder as proof.

To offset the creation of the legend of MacBean, another legend died that July day. Bonnie Dundee was killed in the single volley fired by the government troops. Some said it was a silver bullet which pierced his breastplate, forged from a button and fired by his own servant.

The Prince's Flower

Prior to raising the Jacobite standard at Glenfinnan,

in 1745, Prince Charles journeyed to the Western Isles on a reconnaissance mission. *La Doutelle*, the French frigate which carried him, was buffeted by typical Hebridean weather, but managed to cruise close to the island of Eriskay. Tradition claims that it was Charles himself who decided to land on the island.

There is something dramatic in the image of the young Charles Stuart sitting in the stern of a foreign longboat as he was rowed to one of the most isolated corners of the realm he hoped to inherit. The surge of the Atlantic and the screaming of dozens of seabirds as the boat crept to the tiny, beautiful island is a sad picture with the knowledge of hindsight of the doomed nature of the expedition.

But Charles had no such preordained information.

The longboat was steered to a small inlet where Charles landed, known ever since as *Coilleag d'Phrionnso* (the Prince's Strand), and as he stepped ashore Charles sprinkled flower seeds from his pocket. Where the seeds fell, sprouted lovely pink convolvulus, known to this day as the 'Prince's Flower'. These flowers are believed to wither if transplanted outside Eriskay.

Apart from convolvulus, the prince brought something else to Eriskay, which definitely does not wither outside the island. It was on Eriskay that Drambuie was first drunk, but the Mackinnons of Skye were given the recipe for this liqueur. This was in gratitude for their help when Charles was sheltering after Culloden. It was probably all the prince could offer. The recipe was passed down, ensuring that at least one legacy of the royal Stuarts has been preserved.

Culloden

This, the last pitched battle to be fought on Scottish soil, on 16 April 1746, has been the subject of more myths – and not a few legends – than any other. There is the myth that it was a battle between Scot and Englishman, the legend of the young Wolfe who refused to shoot a wounded Highlander, the myth that the Jacobite clans were eager to fight for their 'Young Pretender', the legend of Gillies MacBean

11

who killed 14 redcoats, and of Big John MacGillivray who disposed of a further 12 with his broadsword.

Culloden is an uneasy place even now. Some people have told of strange sights on the short heather with its all-encroaching forestry and weathered monuments to the dead. The atmosphere is as forbidding as any of the fabled fields of Flanders, for this was where a dream died, where the culture of the Gael received a paralysing blow from which it took generations, centuries, to recover. With the current re-emergence of Gaelic schools throughout Scotland and the introduction of a trickle of money into Gaeldom, there is at last a glimmer of light at the end of a long dark tunnel.

This slough was not caused by Culloden, but the battle had tremendous significance. Culloden and its aftermath killed hope in the Gael. No wonder there were myths told and heroes created to keep some pride in a culture under threat from all sides. After Culloden the martial spirit of the Gael was only allowed to flow under strict supervision, fighting the battles of its conqueror.

Examining the myths one by one, some of the truth can be seen dimly through the fog of battle – or such truth as can survive two and a half centuries of self-delusion and official propaganda. Of the government's 9000 men, around a quarter were Scots – including two battalions of Highlanders – and other clans were in arms for King George II (1683–1760). Prince Charles, born and bred in Continental Europe, did not intend to re-establish an independent Scotland; his idea was to replace George II with James, the Old Pretender, on the British throne – a James whose Roman Catholicism would have found no approval among the Presbyterian mass of Scots. And although Bonnie Prince Charlie's army was largely Highland there were also Lowland Scots, Irish, French and English among its tartan ranks. Highlanders bore the brunt of battle and were treated abominably in the aftermath, but it was the Irish and Lowland Scots, regular regiments in French service, which were the last to leave the field. Although, no doubt at all, there would be some Highlanders in those ranks too.

James Wolfe (1727–59) was to become a hero as he died upon the plains of Abraham, in Canada, 13 years after Culloden. History has been generous to him, portraying him as refusing to shoot a wounded clansman at Culloden despite a direct order from Cumberland himself. The wounded Highlander was Charles Fraser of Inverallochie, commander of the Fraser clan regiment, and Wolfe is reputed to have offered his commission instead of murdering the injured man. Cumberland – if it was he – soon found somebody else to butcher Fraser.

This incident is often used to portray the humanity of Wolfe, but that quality was sadly lacking when, a few years later, he proposed a massacre of the MacPhersons.

Wolfe has been given some credit for reviving the idea of raising regiments of Highlanders to fight for the government, partly because the hillmen were hardy, mainly, one suspects, because they were expendable. It was a regiment of Frasers who clambered up the steep slope to fight his final battle on the plains of Abraham. Among the redcoated soldiers would be men who had fought against him at Culloden, pressed for both wars for different kings by the inexorable rule of clan.

For the clansmen at Culloden were not all eager volunteers. As the pressgang collected men for service in the government's army, the clan chief had measures as harsh to collect his fighting tail. Even the chiefs were unwilling to fight for Bonnie Prince Charlie. Of an estimated Highland strength of 30000 broadswords, no more than 10000 fought for Charlie, and less than 5000 at Culloden. The majority of these possibly came willingly but a sizeable minority did not; threats of house-burnings were used by the 'Gentle' Lochiel, chief of clan Cameron, as well as by Lord Lewis Gordon and MacDonald of Keppoch.

Men were dragged from their beds, intimidated by whip and sword or the loss of their cattle. Those who refused clan conscription faced the anger of their chief; those who came faced the government grapeshot or the fury of Cumberland. Caught between two millstones, there was no escape for the Highlander of 1745.

Maybe 4000 Jacobite Highlanders were present at Culloden, and there were heroes among them. Of all the clans it was the confederation of Chattan who did most damage to the redcoats. They charged to the rant of the pipes and into grapeshot and musketry which killed most before they reached the red ranks. Eighteen of Chattan's 21 officers died there and no doubt the men suffered in proportion, but some still reached the Royal Scots and Cholmondeley's regiment and hacked through them to the infantry in support.

There was six-feet-four Gillies MacBean who survived half a dozen bayonet wounds, a sword slash and a thigh smashed by artillery; he was felled by the second line. He lived through this, withdrew with the rest to hold a gap in the dyke and killed 14 dragoons before he was cut down and trampled. MacGillivray of Dunmaglass also crashed through the first redcoat line but no further, while another MacGillivray killed 12 redcoats before being shot. Yet a third of the same name, Robert Mor, fought with a plough coulter, felling seven redcoats before he too was shot.

If the generalship had been equal to the valour of the Jacobite infantry there might have been a different story to tell of Culloden, but is that not true of too many battles in which Scots have participated, from the defeat at Halidon Hill to the panicked surrender of Singapore?

Charlie and Flora

In Portree, the principal town of the Isle of Skye, there stands a church dedicated to Saint Columba. When the sun is in the correct quarter, the rays will brighten a stained-glass window showing Esther, who became queen of Assyria and saved the Jews from slaughter, in her various guises, underneath the arms of MacDonald and the biblical quote 'If I perish, I perish' (Esther 4,16).

Two miles from the ancient castle of Duntulm, in the same island of Skye, a white Celtic cross throws its message of Christianity over to the Little Minch and the Western Isles. In the hallowed soil beneath the cross, shrouded in the sheet which once graced Prince Charles, a woman lies who was made famous by a boat trip, a walk and a good store of courage.

That woman is part of the pride of Skye and one reason why the Jacobite legends did not die amidst

the carnage of Culloden. Her name was Flora
Macdonald (1722–90) and the stained-glass window
in Saint Columba's church is to honour her memory.

After Culloden, with the glens being savaged by
redcoats, Charles Stuart alternated between hiding
and fleeing. Leaving the mainland, he was taken to
the Outer Isles in an open boat and wandered those
magical, weather-taunted islands while his chosen
country suffered. Even here Charles was not safe,
with government troops and the royal navy engaged
in combined operations to find him. On 21 June
1746, in the island of South Uist, Charles came face
to face with Flora Macdonald.

At this time Flora was 23 years old and, as was to
be proved, very resourceful. There must have been
a conflict of loyalties for Flora, whose stepfather
commanded a regiment of government militia, but
she agreed to escort the prince to Skye. Then began
a series of adventures for the young Uist girl.

First came arrest for having no passport: a
deficiency rectified by her stepfather, who had her
released. Soon after, with the help of Lady Clan-
ranald, Flora made a flowered gown for Charles, for
he was to be disguised as Betty Burke, a servant
girl. Together with the now almost forgotten Neil
MacEachan, they set off in a six-oared boat from
Benbecula to Skye.

A storm made the Little Minch dangerous but
there was no refuge at Vaternish Point, their chosen
landing place. Instead there were redcoats. Musketry
drove Flora on, across the wide waters of Loch
Snizort to Monkstadt. While Charles waited nearby,
tossing stones into the sea, Flora marched to
Monkstadt House and another shock.

As well as Lady Margaret there was an officer of
militia in the house, a regiment camped not far
away. Flora and Lady Margaret engaged the officer in
conversation while Alexander Macdonald of Kingsburgh left with food for the prince – who was
ungrateful enough to attack him with a stick.
Kingsburgh House was the next objective and they
made an interesting spectacle on the road: the
Highland gentleman, the wary MacEachan, young
Flora and the tall prince in a floral gown and
petticoats.

Charles was not very expert at managing his

15

clothes, either letting the dress trail through the many burns, or raising his petticoats revealingly high, much to Flora's consternation. At Kingsburgh, Charles hugged Flora, placed his head in her lap and asked her to cut a lock from his hair – he, a royal prince, had nothing left to give.

Next day they left Kingsburgh, Charles changing back into more manageable clothes and heading for Portree. Flora and Neil aimed for the Isle of Raasay. Unfortunately they had no boat, but there was one on Loch Fada, two miles inland. After being dragged to the coast, the boat had to be lowered over a cliff to the sea. Perhaps, as she gasped with the rough wood, slipped over rock and heather, Flora was glad her prince was not there to see her.

Charles was collected at Portree and there he parted from Flora. He had months of wandering in front of him before his eventual escape to France: Flora had an even more interesting life. Destined to marry the son of Macdonald of Kingsburgh, an officer in the government army, Flora would emigrate to America, returning to Skye when her husband was captured by the rebellious colonials.

There is a story that her homeward-bound ship was attacked by an American privateer and the crew panicked, but again Flora showed her mettle, encouraging the crew to fight until the Americans were repelled.

As enduring as the semi-romance of Bonnie Prince Charlie and Flora is the legend of the reward. Thirty thousand pounds was offered for the capture of the prince, a reward which was never claimed.

Some modern historians have cast doubt on the famed loyalty of the Highlanders, pointing to Highland spies working for the Hanoverians; indeed, such people did exist. However, for all Charles's wanderings, for all the many, many impoverished and endangered Highlanders who met him, sheltered him, knew or at least suspected who he was, the prince was never betrayed. That surely is testimony enough.

The King O'er the Water

In England when Charles II was in exile and Cromwell protected the country and its religion, ardent royalists banded into an organization known as the Sealed Knot and dedicated themselves to fight for his return. This society was largely ineffectual. In Scotland after the 1745 there was no such group.

However, gentlemen of Jacobite persuasion did meet in secret to perform strange rituals. Toasts, supposedly loyally drunk to King George II (1683–1760), were only drunk after the glass was passed above a jug of water, signifying the king referred to was 'over the water' (ie abroad). Later, after the fire of rebellion had been snuffed by redcoat boots, Jacobite meetings were again held, but as no more than a supposedly romantic memory. By that time the manpower of the Highlands was being drained to the government's Continental and colonial escapades and the clan system was no longer viable. There was no danger to George.

There was even less danger to Victoria who, it has been claimed, boasted of Jacobite sympathies herself. And why not, Charles was a relative of her own.

Somewhere, it is said, there is still a Jacobite claimant to the British throne. However, few Scots, if any at all, would welcome a return to a Stuart – or pseudo-Stuart – dynasty.

Supernatural Scotland

Until the 16th century, Europe embraced Christianity with little division, if with differing degrees of enthusiasm. Pockets of paganism survived, and areas of so-called heresy, but from Norway to Sicily the doctrines of the Roman Catholic Church were dominant. Then came Martin Luther, Calvin and their compatriots; their challenge introduced reforms to the depreciating Church, doubt into a stagnating faith and other, older practices spread like cancer amidst people no longer certain. Throughout Europe witchcraft, or rites cursed with that name by worried authorities, spread. Governments attempted to suppress this new evil with the ducking stool and the stake while among the commonalty, people looked askance at the sight of a cat or an old woman with herbal knowledge.

Although many of the charges levelled were patently false, not all the victims were innocent. Perhaps King James VI (1566–1625) had reason for his fear of sorcery, if this legend from North Berwick has any truth in it . . .

The Witches of North Berwick

On 1 May 1590 King James VI was returning from Denmark with his young bride, Princess Anne of Denmark (1574–1619). In Scotland there was devilry, with all the witches of East Lothian called to the old kirk of North Berwick on the shore of the Forth.

Two hundred gathered, of all ages and occupations, from Doctor Fian (whose real name was John Cunningham), the schoolmaster of Saltpans, to aged Agnes Sampson of Keith. At the head of the gathering was the devil himself – or perhaps it was Francis Stewart, the 5th Earl of Bothwell, who was reputed to be a warlock – and he made the witches swear allegiance to him after they kissed his bared buttocks. The devil asked each witch what mischief they had done to the king '. . . the greatest enemie hee hath in the world'. When one old ploughman replied, 'There is naething ails the king yet, God be thankit,' the devil was so annoyed he struck the man. Perhaps the ploughman was not a very dedicated witch.

Others were more serious in their intent. Several graves were desecrated for finger, toe and knee joints, to be pulverized for a spell against the king. Agnes Sampson hung a black toad by the heels, collected the venom which dropped and attempted to smear this on an article of His Grace's clothing. Only the loyalty of James's servant prevented her. Perhaps the venom of a black toad does not sound powerful, but remembering the psychological effect of, for instance, voodoo on a superstitious mind, it could be potent. King James was known to be superstitious.

A cat was caught, baptized and thrown into the sea as a sure method of raising a storm while James was at sea, and the devil threw some spherical object after the cat which, mysteriously, would cause the shipwrecked king to be cast ashore on English, not Scottish, soil.

Fortunately the sorcery failed; James arrived safely in Scotland and in time the witches were summoned to account for their spells. Torture and the purging flame were James's answer to the devil, but perhaps it was William Shakespeare who had the last word when he welcomed King James to England with a play entitled *MacBeth*, in which three witches appeared in the first few pages.

The Brahan Seer

The ability to see into the future, or second sight, is not unique to Scotland but there are many recorded instances throughout Scottish history. A man or woman possessing second sight is known as a seer and one of the best known is Coinneach Odhar – Kenneth the Sallow, known as the Brahan Seer.

Kenneth's birthplace is usually given as Lewis, but he achieved fame after he started working as a labourer – or something similar – on the Brahan estate, Maryburgh, near Dingwall. Like most Scottish seers, Kenneth never achieved – nor probably sought – wealth, and his prophesies were not controlled: he just 'saw'. His birth and death are uncertain, even the period in which he lived, but the 17th century is considered his time. It is possible that a collection of prophesies by different people were bracketed together under his name, but Kenneth is undoubtedly based on a real person.

Round about 1660 Kenneth foretold, 'The time will come when full-rigged ships with sails unfurled will be seen sailing east and west by the back of Tomnahurich Hill.' This was fulfilled in 1822, when Thomas Telford's Caledonian Canal connected the chain of lochs in the Great Glen.

Another prophesy was proved correct in less dramatic fashion when progress brought roads to the once trackless Highlands. 'The day is coming when there will be a ribbon on every hill and a bridge on every stream.' Simple enough stuff perhaps, little more than inspired guesswork caused by watching the advance of commerce in the Lowlands. The same cannot be said of another, disturbing prediction.

Walking over Drummossie Moor he stopped and, apparently in front of witnesses, said: 'This bleak moor, ere many generations have passed, shall be stained with the best blood of Scotland.' In 1746 the battle of Culloden was fought on Drummossie. 'Glad am I that I will not see that day,' Kenneth had said; he was right to be glad.

Not long after the Restoration, according to legend, the Earl of Seaforth, Kenneth's employer, left Scotland for Paris, leaving his wife at Brahan Castle. When the countess heard rumours of Seaforth's behaviour she sent for Kenneth and asked him to confirm them. Until he was pressed, Kenneth refused to say more than 'your Lord is well and merry', but when the countess persisted he revealed that Seaforth was 'on his knees before a fair lady, his arms round her waist, and her hand pressed to his lips'.

Instead of being grateful for the knowledge she had desired, the countess accused Kenneth of witchcraft and ordered him burned in a tar barrel. In response, Kenneth foresaw the downfall of the House of Seaforth, a prophesy which came true in the early 1800s.

One of the most important of Kenneth's sayings

has, until now, only partially come true. There is more than one variation, but among the most popular says, 'The clans will become so effeminate as to allow themselves to be driven from their native land by an army of sheep,' but after that 'the sheep will be gone and so well forgotten that a man finding a jaw bone in a cave will not recognize it or be able to tell what animal it belongs to . . . Strange merchants will take away the land of the great clan chiefs and the mountains will become one wide deer forest . . . the people forced to seek shelter in far-away islands.'

This has happened, with the Highlanders being evicted to make way for sheep farms which in turn have become vacant sporting estates owned by non-Scots. It is the second half of the prophesy which is disturbing:

> Then will come the time of the horrid Black Rains. They will kill the deer and wither the grass. Weep for the mountains . . . weep for the wilderness of the Gael. After that, long, long after, the people will return and take possession of the land of their ancestors.

Perhaps the black rain is nuclear fallout, or a way of pointing out the pollution caused by the oil industry. Interestingly, black rain fell on southern Iran and Kuwait during the Gulf War. The rebirth of Gaeldom is encouraging, but after Culloden and the Clearances, perhaps it is better not to speculate on the prophesies of Coinneach Odhar. Not for nothing do people who have the sight term it a curse, and could he really forsee the nightmare of burning oilwells which created Kuwait's own brand of black rain?

Major Weir

When the great Montrose was executed – at a cost to Edinburgh of 32 pounds and four pence – the leader of his escort was one Major Weir (c.1600–70). Stern-faced, big-nosed and dressed in black, Weir looked the model of an extreme Presbyterian as he stalked the crowded city streets, his cloak undulating in the wake of his passage. In his hand he clutched a black, carved staff. Montrose, gallant,

21

egotistical, a cavalier to the end, found no sympathy from the major, who taunted him on the road to his death. 'Dog,' Weir called him, 'atheist and murderer.'

Strong words from an elder of the Kirk – to ease a guilty conscience perhaps? For all was not what it seemed with the major of the guard. He lived in the West Bow of Edinburgh, a street which at that time wound tightly from the bustling Grassmarket to the Royal Mile, a street of tall tenements and claustrophobic closes, of stone cobbles greasy with filth and the choking smoke from a thousand chimneys. A number of 'Bowhead Saints' – strict Presbyterians – lived here, and knew Weir as 'Angelic Thomas', so severe was his bond to the Kirk. In his dark cloak and carrying his staff, Weir was a man to respect.

Then, in 1670, Weir revealed the truth about himself. He became ill, not uncommon in the Edinburgh which merited its title of 'Auld Reekie', and confessed to being a warlock, to serving Satan, to having an incestuous relationship with his sister Grizel, and to bestiality.

Not wishing to believe such things of a Kirk elder, his fellows blamed his illness for the weird fantasies. Soon, however, people began to point malicious fingers. They had seen his staff walking in front of the major, and it had the power to knock on doors. Not only that, but the sermons for which Weir was famous came from that same source; that staff was the fountainhead of all the major's powers.

After that there was only one thing to do. He was arrested and tried. On 12 April 1670 Major Weir was burned at the stake between Edinburgh and Leith. The staff was burned also, and it twisted and writhed in the flames. Weir's sister Grizel, who had also confessed, saying that she and Weir used to drive in a flaming coach to Musselburgh to meet the devil, suffered death by hanging. Grizel created a scandal by attempting to strip off her clothes before being executed. Public hangings were all very well but public nudity was downright immoral in the prim Edinburgh of that time.

If the god-fearing citizens of the capital thought that was the last of Major Weir, they were mistaken. For long after his death the major haunted his old house, making it impossible to lease or sell. On the odd occasion, the devil himself came to visit, rattling down the West Bow in a black coach drawn by six headless horses. Who knows, perhaps he still does?

The Witch of Badenoch

Deep in the heart of Scotland, the district of Badenoch stretches from Loch Laggan to Cairngorm, from Atholl to the Monadhliach mountains. Not far from the source of Spey, the farm of Laggan is central in Badenoch, sitting in the shade of Marg na Craige. It is a peaceful place now, except for the traffic on the A86 and the chatter of visitors from the centres of Aviemore and Newtonmore. It was not always so.

A long time ago Laggan was the home of a lady known as Bean an Lagain (Wife of Laggan) who had the reputation of being a witch. Nowadays it is possible to laugh at such an estimation, but in the past a witch was an object of genuine fear. The Highlands would have been a lonely place, at the whim of every caprice of tyrannical nature, isolated by gaunt mountains and deep forests, by passes made impenetrable by snow, and glens which were boggy or barren.

Superstition was rife, based on a mixture of ignorance and ancient beliefs warped by half-remembered knowledge. Amongst this lived a people naturally imaginative, laced with individuals blessed (or cursed) with powers denied to most. In a

23

land where lochs could host water-horses, seas concealed mermaids and standing stones evoked powerful images from the past, was witchcraft so unimaginable?

The Wife of Laggan lived in a state of continuous feud with her neighbours in the township of Taigh na Camaisidh and when the nearest crofter found the Wife's sheep loose among his fields he was not surprised. Angrily he penned them, refusing to give them back to the Wife until she paid for the damage they had caused. This backfired, for the Wife began a campaign of attrition against the crofter. A series of misfortunes drove the man out of Badenoch and as he left he muttered about the great black cat which had plagued him.

For a while the croft remained empty but others in the township suffered the wrath of the Wife, with animals sickening, crops failing and minor accidents becoming too commonplace to be coincidence. At length the township fought fire with fire as one Donald Bane took over the vacant croft. Donald was a bit of a witch himself, of the white variety, and he knew what measures could counter the Wife's attacks.

Bog fir tied to the tail or horn of a cow protected the animal from sorcery, while an iron horseshoe, or a rowan branch tied into the shape of a cross, could be placed above a door or window to deny access to anything evil. With the buildings secure and animals safe, the folk of Taigh na Camaisidh could breathe easier, but there was still a black cat creeping around, hens and eggs were still vanishing. It was not practical in those free-ranging days to keep all the fowl indoors. Donald, however, had the answer.

Melting a spoon for silver, Donald moulded a bullet and went hunting for the cat. A sighting, a quick shot followed by a very human scream and when next seen the Wife of Laggan was limping. She also knew how dangerous her opponent was.

Autumn came early to Badenoch, bringing rain from the west. Working at the summer shieling, Donald was at his fireside, drying his clothes when a black hen fluttered to his feet. This was no bird of his, so Donald blessed himself. Gradually the hen grew larger, altering shape until it became the Wife of Laggan crouching by Donald's fire. On the opposite side of the flames, Donald's dogs growled and snarled, hackles rising, but they were too well trained to attack unless ordered. Not knowing this, the Wife was nervous, and asked Donald to tie them.

'I'm sorry,' Donald replied, shaking his head, 'but I've no rope.'

The Wife smiled, pulled out some of her long hair and suggested he use that instead. Wary of the Wife, Donald appeared to tie back his dogs but instead fastened the hair round his coat sleeve.

Sure of the success of her plan, the Wife attacked him, screaming: 'Tighten hair, cut and strangle.' Instead of choking the dogs, the hair tightened round Donald's coat.

When the dogs saw their master in danger they leaped on the Wife, throwing her to the polished earth floor. She screamed, struggled and ran, with both dogs snapping at her. Donald remained in the shieling all night, only leaving when dawn arrived.

There was a dead dog on the track, choked by the piece of bloody flesh in its mouth. Other men of the township joined Donald and told him that the Wife was dying. Donald's dogs had gnawed and bitten her so badly that she would not survive long. One by one the crofters joined Donald as he walked to Laggan, but they remained at the door as he entered the witch's farm.

They took the body of the witch to the top of a knoll and there they burned it. That knoll – Witch Hill – was marked by nature, for no trees grow above the ashes of the Wife of Laggan.

Religious Legends

For as far back as records go, and probably much further, Scotland has been a religious country. The land, mainland and islands, is scattered with religious foundations, mostly ruinous but by no means all. In Lewis the Standing Stones of Callanish, where the mysterious Shining Ones are said to appear at midsummer, could have had religious connotations, while hermits' cells from the Dark Ages precede the great medieval abbeys of the Lowlands. And everywhere, from the most northerly isle to the Rhinns of Galloway, the small, solid kirks stand four-square and dour against climate and unenlightenment alike.

With such a background and with a people much given to theological contention, it was only natural that legends about the saints should abound in Scotland. There are many such saints who have had a claim on the Scottish psyche; most have been laid aside with the passage of time and survive only in names of the places they once inhabited. Others have remained part of daily life: Andrew, who met the Christ; Columba, statesman and missionary of Dalriada; Mungo, Glasgow's own saint; and Margaret, who helped guide the nation back to the mainstream of European Christianity. There is even a legend that Pontius Pilate was born in Scotland.

Saint Andrew

Many miles separate the beach at Capernaum from the sands of eastern Fife but they are united for ever by the name of a saint. Andrew was a fisherman on the Sea of Galilee; he met Jesus, abandoned the search for fish and became one of the original 12 disciples. Preaching the word, Andrew trod the dusty roads of the eastern Roman Empire for three decades before being martyred at Patras in Greece. Legend says that his persecutors were about to crucify him on a cross fashioned like that on Calvary,

26

but Andrew said he was not worthy of such an honour and instead was hung upside down on a Saltire-shaped cross. Both Greece and Russia later adopted Andrew as their patron saint.

The Scottish connection begins seven centuries later, when a ship from Patras was driven by a storm to the shore of Fife and one of the survivors, a monk named Rule or Regulus, landed. Rule stated that an angel had ordered him to carry relics of Saint Andrew to Scotland. The relics were bones: an arm bone, a knee-cap, one tooth and three fingers of a long-dead man, but such things were venerated throughout the Dark and Middle Ages. A church was built round the bones and the settlement, after being Muckross, Kilrymont and Kilrule, became known as Saint Andrews.

Another version of the legend puts the shipwreck as early as the fourth century AD. Despite the probable pagan nature of Pictish Fife at the time, this date seems more plausible, because by the eighth century there were no longer any of Andrew's bones remaining in Patras; they had been transported to Constantinople in AD 357. Perhaps one load went as far astray as Fife. Or could it be that the monk shipwrecked in the land of King Angus only claimed his cargo consisted of holy bones; forgeries were not unheard of in the Dark Ages.

Rule is well remembered in St Andrews, with a church and tower dedicated to him. The church, small and solid, is older than the Norman encroachment, its narrow windows perfectly suited for Scotland's wind-buffeted east coast. The church's tower has a resident ghost – a friendly monk who guides the weary up the interior steps.

Whatever bones Saint Rule brought to Fife are no longer in St Andrews. After the Cromwellian invasion of Scotland in 1648, the Lord Protector encouraged the townspeople of St Andrews to quarry the remains of the cathedral for building stone. What appears blatant vandalism in the 20th century was only common sense in the 17th, and the subsequent disappearance of the holy bones is not to be wondered at. However, Bishop Francis Thomson of Motherwell brought two relics of St Andrew from Amalfi; one is housed in St Mary's Cathedral, Edinburgh, the other in St John's in St

Andrews, alongside a further relic given by Pope Paul VI in 1969.

Saint Columba

Scotland had not yet been named and of all the peoples who form component parts of her, two had not yet arrived. The Picts were here, as they – or their ancestors – had been for centuries. The Britons of Strathclyde were here, uneasily watching a long border with still-pagan Angles, and in the splintered islands west of Strathclyde and south of the Picts, the Gaels had penetrated, the race known as Scotti (Scots).

Western Scotland and Northern Ireland share aspects of a common heritage, common bloodlines and, in many cases, common failings. The Cruithin (Picts) of Scotland were surely related to the Cruithin of Ulster, Clan Donald owned the Antrim glens as surely as they owned Kintyre and Islay, and of the 17th-century colonists 'planted' in Northern Ireland, a great many came from Scotland. As important as any of these movements was the migration of Gaels from Dalriada in Ulster to what was to become Argyll in Scotland.

Fergus Mor MacErc brought 150 Scots, the nucleus of a nation, to the western seaboard of Scotland. Perhaps he had to fight, more likely the Picts allowed him to found the new colony of Dalriada – named after his Irish homeland. Within a few decades, however, there was war between Pict and Scot, and Dalriada was defeated. The royal line remained, the name remained, but Brude, king of the northern Picts, was a major threat to the continuation of the colony.

Back in Ireland there was a priest named Colum, the dove. His other name was Crinthan, the wolf. This priest alternated between both names, using the wolf side of his nature to pursue the Church militant, the dove side to emphasize the gentle nature of Christianity. A member of the royal line of Ui Neill, kings of Tara, Columba was earmarked for fame even before he was born.

Eithne, Columba's mother, dreamed that she was offered a beautiful robe by an angel. As she accepted the garment, the angel snatched it back, and spread it so that the fine wool enveloped the land of Ireland. Too large a cloak for the island, one corner trailed over the sea until it touched Scotland. At once Eithne realized that her son would evangelize hundreds of people.

Brought up for the priesthood, Columba travelled round Ireland founding churches and monasteries, including that of Derry. Exactly why Columba left Ireland for Scotland is uncertain; he seems to have participated in the battle of Guildreimhne, for which the Irish Church excommunicated him. The excommunication was lifted but Columba's guilt remained and he left Ireland for exile into Scotland.

It is also possible that Columba emigrated across the North Channel for no other reason than to strengthen the faith of his beleaguered countrymen. Adamnan, Columba's biographer, gave the latter reason: 'In the forty-second year of his age, desiring to seek a foreign country for the sake of Christ, he sailed from Ireland to Britain.'

Iona, a small island off Mull, became Columba's – and Christianity's – headquarters in Scotland. For two years Columba consolidated his position here: training, farming, organizing. Then came the major challenge: Druidical Pictland.

Always a man of direct action, Columba did not nibble at the edge of Brude's domain. Instead he marched straight to Brude's capital, which was somewhere near Inverness. Today the route is relatively simple but in the sixth century it meant a long and dangerous journey by land and sea, always in peril from wild men in the deep forests. Or perhaps not; the Celts were inveterate wanderers, saints appeared to be more adventurous than most, and danger never seemed to worry them. Either the mantle of the Lord would appear to be in their favour or people from the Dark Ages were more civilized than they are generally given credit for.

Brude, hearing of Columba's coming, closed and bolted the gates of his dun (fortified hill) and waited behind them. Brude was not alone; at his side was Broichan, chief Druid. Politely, Columba requested admittance; not so politely, Brude and Broichan refused. It could have been the end of Columba's evangelical career, but the saint had faith. Making the sign of the cross, he compelled the bolt to withdraw, the gates to burst open, and in he walked.

This miracle, combined with others, discomforted Broichan and impressed Brude so much that – according to legend – he converted to Christianity. Columba's skills included singing; his loud rendering of Psalm 45, 'My heart overflows with a goodly theme', silenced the Druids, while his commands forced a great monster from Loch Ness to sink into the dark water. It re-emerged later, however, in the 1930s.

Not as dramatic as his miracles but psychologically possibly even more important was the coronation by Columba of Aedan MacGabrain. This was the first coronation in Britain and established the power of the Church to make kings. The semi-divine nature of kingship was altered from a mainly pagan to a partly Christian divinity; Church and state combined in a powerful coalition which still, to an extent, exists today.

Columba was as much a statesman as a saint.

Saint Mungo

Mungo, or Kentigern, is as closely associated with urban Glasgow as Columba is with Iona. He was born around AD 527, his mother a pagan princess, his grandfather a British king. How many of the saints were of royal descent? Often overlooked is the education of these early missionaries: who taught the teachers? In Mungo's case it was Servanus of

Culross in Fife – interestingly close to the supposed landing site of Andrew's bones.

Fully educated and dedicated to Christianity, Mungo (from the Brythonic Muncho, 'dear friend') travelled west, stopping to converse with a hermit named Fergus. There was a prophesy that Fergus would not die until he had seen Mungo, so he must have had mixed feelings as the saint came into view. After meeting the missionary, Fergus dutifully passed away. This fulfilled the prophesy admirably but left Mungo with a body on his hands. Carefully placing Fergus on a conveniently handy cart, Mungo rounded up a pair of wild bulls and yoked them on to the vehicle. This done, he ordered the bulls to haul away.

The bulls stopped at an unused cemetery which St Ninian had consecrated hundreds of years earlier – conversion was a time-consuming operation in old Scotland – and here Fergus was buried.

In time, Glasgow Cathedral would be built on this site.

That was only the beginning of Mungo's Glasgow connection. A resurgence of paganism forced the saint to Wales until the north stabilized. Rhydderich Hen, Christian King of Strathclyde and conqueror of a pagan force at the battle of Arderydd in 573, invited Mungo back to Strathclyde, and Mungo returned to the Molindar Burn where Fergus was buried. This time he remained, being visited by his contemporary, Columba, who presented him with a crozier. Such a meeting must have given a great boost to the spirituality of the place, already known as Glesgu – Mungo's 'Dear green place'.

The saints were not great builders so Mungo's religious foundation would have been of wood and wattle, although he might have had a stone chapel, or beehive cells like those existing in Eileach Naoimh on the Garvellach Islands. From this small establishment Mungo spread the gospel. As could be expected with a superstitious people, tales of Mungo's miracles became current, one even reaching down the centuries to be enshrined in the arms of Glasgow.

Rhydderich's queen, Languoreth, had formed a friendship with one of the king's handsome young knights. This annoyed Rhydderich, particularly when Languoreth presented the knight with a ring he had given her.

Calling his retinue out for a hunt, Rhydderich led them from his capital at Dumbarton to his hunting seat at the Mote Hill near Cadzow. Here they rested and Rhydderich removed his ring from the finger of the sleeping knight and tossed it into the Clyde.

This was only the start of the royal rage, for Rhydderich sent for his wife and commanded her to return the ring. 'And if I cannot, sire?' she asked, eyes downcast.

'Then I cut off your head,' he told her. Or something equally unpleasant. In such a predicament what could the queen do but run to the nearest saint for help?

Mungo had a simple solution. Sending one of his monks to the Clyde, he told him to cast for a fish and haul out the first one he caught. The man did so, and brought a fine salmon to the saint. 'Excellent,' said Mungo, reached into the mouth of the fish and brought out the missing ring.

Not only the fish, but the ring and Mungo's bell are on the city's coat of arms, as well as a bush he set aflame with the name of the Holy Trinity. Mungo, the saint of Strathclyde.

Saint Margaret

With the great contribution women have made to the continuing story of Scotland, it would be totally inappropriate not to include Saint Margaret (c.1046–93) in any collection of saints. Unlike Columba and Mungo, she was no worker of dramatic miracles but in her own way she worked wonders in a Scotland still more than half savage.

One charge often levied at Margaret is that, in encouraging the advent of Norman ways and Roman Catholicism, she undermined both the native culture and the native Columban Church. There is truth in this, but like so much else in Scotland's past, it is a distorted truth. Margaret was no friend of the Normans, quite the reverse. Her father was a nephew of Edward the Confessor of England and had lived in exile in passionately Christian Hungary. Here Margaret had been born and raised, imbued with piety and goodness. After the Normans

32

defeated Saxon England, Margaret fled north.

At a place on the Firth of Forth now known as St Margaret's Hope, Margaret and her companions landed and were met by the Scottish king, Malcolm Canmore. It was a storybook romance: the young, lovely, learned and pious princess and the travelled, intelligent Scottish king.

Soon after their marriage in the Columban church in Dunfermline, Margaret, supported by Malcolm, began to restructure and modernize the Scottish Church. Dunfermline was rebuilt and, possibly more significant, so was the monastery at Iona which had fallen into disrepair due to Norse raids and simple neglect. Margaret did not demolish the old Celtic church and sternly impose Catholicism; the Celtic church was decaying – partly through no fault of its own – and continued to decay. In its day it had been vigorous, forward-looking and evangelistic, but that day was largely past. Instead Margaret moved Scotland into the mainstream of European Christianity in a manner more gentle than the 16th-century reformers did when they replaced the likewise rotting Catholic Church with the Protestant variety.

As well as St Margaret's Hope, there is Queensferry to remind Scotland of the saint. Margaret often travelled between Fife and Lothian, and the ferry, which probably predated her, was named in her honour. Today the passage is spanned by the famous bridges.

Equally historic but more tangible is St Margaret's

Chapel in Edinburgh Castle. As the oldest building in the capital, the chapel has enough claim to fame; as a permanent reminder of the queenly saint it is doubly enhanced, yet this tiny building, holding only 26 people when crammed full, is more than that. As precious as Iona in its own way, the atmosphere is unique.

The greatest legacy Margaret has left Scotland, however, is the memory of a saint. At a time when England was ruled by the ruthless William, whose kingdom was immersed in a welter of blood, Scotland's queen is remembered for piety and humility. The enduring picture is of a great queen on her knees, washing the feet of the poor.

Pontius Pilate

Gracing the village of Fortingall in Glen Lyon, Perthshire, is a yew tree which has endured some 3000 Scottish winters. This is an incredible span, difficult to comprehend in years alone. Perhaps it would be easier to say that the tree was there when the Philistines were holding down the Hebrews by denying them the new invention of iron, and it was 2000 years old when Magnus Barelegs crossed from West to East Loch Tarbert on his Viking galley to claim Kintyre for himself.

So this tree was no youngster when a small party of Romans, penetrating far beyond their imperial frontier, entered the glen. Caesar Augustus, basking in sunny Rome, had decided to send peace envoys to all the nations which lay outside the empire.

At this time, with the Romans no closer to yet unnamed Scotland than Gaul, it must have been an unpopular posting, so far away into the unknown, very pagan and extremely cold north. Yet perhaps for aspiring young officers it afforded a chance of recognition and an opportunity to escape from military discipline for a while.

The Romans, however, were nothing if not tenacious and some brave men made the journey. It is unlikely they came by land all the length of Britain; perhaps a galley dropped them off in the upper Forth or in the Tay around Perth. However they arrived, King Mettalanus greeted them hospitably.

Mettalanus, an ancestor of clan Menzies – or so that clan claims – is supposed to have had his seat at Dun Geal, a small, barren hillfort which glowers down at Fortingall from an altitude of a few hundred feet. This could have been a stronghold in time of war, but there are remnants of a much larger fort beneath the rocky summit, more suitable as a permanent capital.

Either negotiations took longer than anticipated, or the emissary's timing was out, for he was obliged to spend the winter with Mettalanus. Coming from the Mediterranean, a Highland winter must have been a shock, with its driving snow, biting cold winds and long, long dark nights. However, there were compensations. Allegedly, Pictish women did not form lasting relationships, they had their choice of men, and Mettalanus had no objection to some of them helping the Romans through the winter.

At last spring released the Romans from their confinement and, with varying memories of their visit, they embarked on the long journey home. They did not travel alone: one of the Pictish ladies had fallen pregnant during the Roman's protracted stay and she gave birth to her son before they left. Thus was born the first Scottish-Italian and his name was destined to fame – or rather notoriety. He was called Pontius Pilate.

Could there be any truth in this legend? Surely the very fact of its improbability tends to lend it credence, as does its durability. The historian Holinshed mentions this story back in the 16th century, and he was quoting from earlier writings. It is unfortunate that the only man from Scotland to be in the text of the Bible had the task of ordering the crucifixion, but he had little choice in the matter and he did his job fairly and with some compassion. Did he not attempt to divert the crowd's anger to another? Pilate is the first recorded Scottish soldier, but the Roman legions were to meet his relations shortly.

There is another connection between Pilate and Scotland, of more modern date. The Royal Scots, the oldest regiment in the British army, were arguing about their antiquity with the Picardy Regiment of France. The Picardy Regiment boasted: 'We guarded the tomb of Christ,' but the Royal Jocks had a quick reply: 'If we had done that job, he wouldn't have escaped so easily. At that time we were Pontius Pilate's bodyguard.'

That label stuck, but the boast had more than a little truth in it. The Royal Scots have played a notable part in too many campaigns for anything they do or say to be discounted.

Royal Legends

Royalty has always inspired legends; how many tales are there of handsome princes and beautiful princesses? Scotland is no exception to this rule with many of her long line of kings and queens being remembered by folk-tales and stories. Some of these are no doubt apocryphal, others true, or based on truth, but all point in some way to the personality of the monarch concerned or to the very fabric of royalty.

What is different about the Scottish legends is the closeness of the monarch to the people; democracy was strong in Scotland from an early age. Perhaps this has something to do with the near constant struggle for national survival of the Scottish nation, or just the demanding character of the Scottish people. It would be hard to be autocratic to a man wielding a lochaber axe, particularly if his clan was eager to back him up.

Both the chosen legends here illustrate this point. Alexander III was not too kingly for the master of the salt works to give him brotherly advice, while Robert Bruce, the most famous of all Scottish kings, was human enough to take refuge in a cave and contemplate the work of a spider. There is a lesson here for all who would seek to rule.

The Stone of Destiny

Sunlight fell on polished armour, heraldic symbols emblazoned silken surcoats, destriers pawed at the muddy ground: these were the signs of victory as the conquerors rode into the old stone abbey. As they advanced, the monks fled, all save Abbot Henry who stood his ground, albeit nervously.

'We have your stone,' a knight said, sidling his charger past the abbot, 'for what it is worth.'

'You have our stone,' the abbot confirmed. He kept his eyes down, not meeting the Englishman's stare. 'Now you may leave.'

There was no reply from the English knight as he led his band away, dragging the stone with them.

Quiet descended on the Abbey of Scone, broken by the chanted prayers of the monks, by the music of a lone blackbird somewhere nearby. There should have been grief, a sense of desecration at the theft of the Lia-fàil, the Stone of Destiny, on which Scottish kings had been ordained for centuries. Instead there was a small smile on the innocent face of the abbot, a spark of laughter in his eyes. For the rough hewn block of sandstone which the English had hauled away was not the Stone of Destiny; the original stone had been hidden on Dunsinane Hill when news of the invasion reached Scone.

There are many legends concerning the stone, not all of them ancient. Possibly the oldest, or the first recorded, tells of its history. Gaythelus, the original Gael, was a Greek prince who brought the stone to Spain. From there the stone travelled to Ireland in the company of Scota, a daughter of the Pharoah. Scota, naturally, was the first Scot.

From this point on there is more of a possibility of fact, considering that some Celts did travel from Spain to Ireland thousands of years before these legends were written down. The stone was used for the coronation of kings in Ireland, perhaps even the High King at Tara (Saint Columba's line), although that is unlikely, and it came over to Scotland with Fergus MacErc in the early sixth century.

The Scots named their colony Dalriada, after their Irish homeland, and centred the kingdom at DunAdd, a prominent, if low, hill conveniently central to the south-west seaboard and passage to Ireland. Here, at DunAdd, the Stone of Destiny presided, sat on by a succession of kings.

As DunAdd expanded the stone was moved, first to Dunstaffnage – or, more accurately, to Dunbeg nearby, an older but less commanding site. Dunstaffnage was not built until the 13th century. Three hundred years or so after Fergus led his band ashore, the stone was transferred to Scone where it was safer from Norse raids. Kenneth MacAlpin, the king who united Scots and Picts, brought the stone here around AD 844 and here it remained for over four centuries.

In 1249 Alexander III, all of seven years old, was placed on the stone and invested with kingly robes. During this ceremony a seannachie recited his pedigree, right back to Gaythelus so long ago, in the old, Gaelic language. Alexander was to be a distinguished king, but the security of the stone was to be imperilled with his untimely death. Edward I's war of 1296 brought confusion to Scotland, and with it the supposed loss of the stone and a hardening of national identity. However, the English, when they carted their worthless sandstone trophy south, were exultant:

> I'll tell you truly what the Stone of Scotland is,
> How Edward King of England has taken it,
> By the Grace of Jesus and by hard fighting,
> To Saint Edward has he given it.

The 'Saint Edward' was Edward the Confessor, a Saxon king of England before the Normans conquered the country. Other rhymes had less religious content:

> Their king's seat of Scone
> is driven over down
> to London led.

Bald words for a bold act and soon the English fabricated their own legends for the stone. It was Jacob's Pillow, they said, or Columba's Pillow and they venerated the crudely carved lump of sandstone which Edward I of England had captured in his Scottish wars. Edward himself was not so sure; only two years after the original raid, he sent a band from Stirling specifically to attack Scone. Admittedly he was engaged in warfare with William Wallace at the time, but it seems an unusual diversion in the middle of a campaign.

The stone in Westminster is 26 inches by 16 inches by 10 inches of sandstone very similar in composition to that near Scone. At either end it has been fitted with iron staples and rings, presumably for carriage, and it weighs one-fifth of a ton. After its removal, Edward ordered a Coronation Chair to be built around it, so that in future English kings could

39

claim to be crowned on the Stone of Destiny, thus strengthening their spurious, if tenaciously adhered to, claim for Scotland. 'Wherever the stone should rest,' the old prophesy said, 'a King of Scots would reign.'

The stone which Edward did not get has been described as ornately carved, shaped like a saddle or a chair and was of marble, or something similar. Possibly it was a meteorite and was used as an altar by one of the early Celtic saints, maybe even by Columba himself – which would make it immensely important, far more so than anything carried from the East.

In Scotland, the war continued, Robert Bruce was crowned king in March 1306, and he might have been sitting on the genuine stone as a MacDuff placed the gold crown on his head. From Scone he moved on, to defeat, hardship and ultimately to victory at Bannockburn and beyond. At Bannock-burn Bruce was joined, so legend claims, by members of the military order of Knights Templar. These warriors were famed for their prowess and perhaps Bruce had a reason for using them at a time when he was short of heavy cavalry and France had turned her back on the order. Did he hand the stone into their keeping after it was retrieved from Dunsinane Hill? It is another theory.

Victory after victory sent the English home and eventually they were forced to make peace. In 1327 the treaty of Edinburgh confirmed the secure independence which Scotland had enjoyed before 1296 and which was all she sought. This treaty made no mention of the stone, which is a significant omission if the English truly held it, and a mistake Bruce was extremely unlikely to make. When, in 1328, the English decided they could restore their version of the stone, the London mob apparently prevented its release. Understandably, the Scots were not concerned: they had the original.

For a long time the stone slipped from the forefront of national consciousness, then, on 26 December 1950, in a world totally changed from the feudalism of the Middle Ages, it became head-line news again. 'Act of Sacrilege' the newspapers proclaimed, or the much milder 'Student Rag'. Four Scottish students had motored down to London, entered Westminster Abbey and removed the sandstone block from beneath Edward I's Coronation Chair.

While Scotland laughed at the fuss made over the theft of a fake, the police searched diligently, and the four nationalist students were busy in a stonemason's yard. A number of copies of the sandstone block were made.

In April 1951 the students informed the police that a stone had been placed on the High Altar of Arbroath Abbey. This abbey, founded by William the Lion, was the scene of the first reading of the Declaration of Independence in 1320. This gives Arbroath an evocative place in Scotland's history, and the removal and replacement of the stone was more than a simple theft: it was a declaration of nationalism.

As the police threw their newfound stone into the boot of a police car and hustled it back to Westminster, the four students must have felt similar emotions to those experienced by Abbot Henry of Scone so long before. Once again a false stone was being taken south. But after all this time, all these happenings, only one thing seems certain: the stone which sits beneath the Coronation Chair of Edward I is not the stone used for the coronation of Kenneth MacAlpin, Alexander III or Robert Bruce. The actions of the four students and of Abbot Henry would make sure of that.

Alexander III

It was March 1286 and a gale blasted at Scotland's east coast. Wind-driven, the waves smashed against the cliff base and retreated in angry frustration to gather strength for the next assault. The rider, hurrying ahead of his companions, hugged the now sodden cloak tight to him and wondered again if he should have come. Kicking with spurred heels, he encouraged his horse to more speed, peered at the castle lights he could see dimly glowing ahead. Not far now, he promised himself, not far to Kinghorn and the waiting arms of his wife.

The horseman was Alexander III (1241–86), conqueror of King Haakon of Norway, king of peaceful, prosperous Scotland. Peaceful, but still endangered, for the king's first son had not survived childhood and his daughter had died in childbirth. That left one other son, and when he died at 20 the Scots parliament had no option but to name the king's granddaughter as heir presumptive.

Any medieval kingdom with an infant monarch was open to interference from her neighbours, particularly if the child was female, so Alexander hurriedly remarried. He was only 45, time yet to make a male heir to ensure the stability of the realm.

Six months after his marriage to Yolande of Dreux, Alexander had to leave her in Kinghorn while he travelled to Edinburgh, across the Forth. Business concluded, the king was about to set off for Yolande when he was warned to stay put. None other than Thomas the Rhymer, a famous seer, predicted, 'Alas for tomorrow, a day of calamity and misery. Before the 12th hour shall be the sorest wind and tempest that ever was heard of in Scotland.'

Perhaps Alexander hesitated; Thomas had a powerful reputation, but the king's wife had an even more powerful allure – they were newly-weds after all – and the king decided to make the journey. Outside, the wind was already rising and its shrieking through the battlements of Edinburgh Castle might have reminded Alexander of another occasion.

The day of his wedding at Jedburgh Abbey and the town filled with noblemen from Scotland and France. Rich silks and velvet, high-bred laughter and nuptial anticipation. There were pipes and harps and lutes, swordsmen displaying their skill, tables piled with food, all lit by flickering torches, then a masked man entered the company.

A mummer, some said, but none were sure who, as the man paraded through the crowd. Dressed as a skeleton and dancing to the music, he came to Alexander where he sat with his new queen, pointed a bony finger at the royal couple. Yolande shuddered, hid her face in cupped hands; the bishop advanced, cross upraised and the skeleton vanished as dramatically as it had appeared. The whole episode left a chill.

Some claimed that the skeleton had been a one-time lover of Yolande, a soldier who shortly after entered Melrose Abbey as a monk and laughed at mention of the masque.

Alexander, however, was also a warrior and no man to be frightened of portents or weird warnings. He took a small escort with him as he rode for the ferry. The ferryman was not keen to chance the choppy water, but hid his fear behind his words: 'I could not die better than in the company of your father's son.'

They landed safely at Inverkeithing, where the master of the salt works, obviously an old friend, advised the king to stay the night. 'How many times have I tried to persuade you that midnight travelling will bring you no good?'

Alexander laughed and rode on, not realizing how long it would be before Scots voices were heard uttering anything other than war-cries.

Not far to Kinghorn and Yolande; Alexander trotted ahead of his companions as the northerly wind tugged at him. He did not make it to his wife. At a stretch of clifftop coastline, only a short distance from the castle, his horse stumbled and the king fell. His body was found next morning, with his neck broken, by a poor Fifer, Murdoch Schanks. Of all Scotland, only that one man profited from the death of the king, for, while he was granted lands for his discovery, the tempest was just around the corner.

There is a Celtic cross to mark the spot where Alexander III fell. A reminder of what might have been if a king had survived.

Robert the Bruce

The tempest came. It came in the shape of Edward I (1239–1307) of England, so-called 'Hammer of the Scots' and one of the worst enemies Scotland has ever had. This world has seen many ogres: Atilla the Hun, Ghengis Khan, Hitler. Scotland has had the misfortune to suffer from three of the worst: Butcher Cumberland, Henry VIII of England and Edward Longshanks, the Hammer.

Before Edward, Scotland and England were neighbours. After Edward they were enemies. The series of wars he started lasted a century, the acrimony he mostly created continues in a measure to the present day.

At a time when Wallace was dead and only his

43

spirit encouraged Scottish resistance to the invader, another leader emerged from the chaos. Robert Bruce (1274–1329) was his name and he claimed royal blood in his veins. Brought up to an earldom, Bruce was part Celt, part Scottish–Norman and he knew Edward of England as a friend. This combination had inspired his grandfather to claim the throne; he failed but the ambition was not forgotten.

Bruce's rival was the Red Comyn, and in the Minorite house in Dumfries the two met to discuss policy. Two ambitious, proud men, they argued, and Bruce stabbed Comyn at the altar. 'I doubt,' Bruce is alleged to have said to his followers, 'I have slain Comyn.'

'You doubt,' fierce Kirkpatrick replied, 'I'll mak siccar [sure].' And entering the church, he finished off the wounded man. From that time on Bruce could not return; he claimed the crown and waged war on the English.

At first it was not a successful war. Shortly after his crowning, Bruce was defeated at Methven. He withdrew west, to be ambushed by pro-Comyn MacDougalls at DalRigh; his followers scattered and he himself only escaped with a handful of men. There was worse to come. His wife and daughter were captured in or near St Duthain's shrine at Tain and imprisoned. The Countess of Buchan, who had crowned him, was placed in a cage in Berwick, and one by one his brothers were captured and murdered. Things could not have been worse for the King of Scots.

Robert Bruce crouched in a cave, a tiny fire serving only to magnify the gloom and despair of the place. From outside came the recurrent boom and suck of surf on a pebble beach, the lonely scream of a gull. Inside it was quiet, save for the constant drip of falling moisture. Bruce moved, easing cramp in one leg, touched the hilt of the sword he constantly wore. Where was he now? Rathlin? That island between Scotland and Ireland, claimed by both, owned by the Gael? Or was he on the west coast of Arran, with the sun sinking on Kintyre across St Brendan's Sound? Bruce shook his head; he might even be in the Galloway hills; it did not matter. He was near defeat.

Rubbing a hand across his face, Bruce felt the rasp

of stubble, the prominence of bone through the gaunt features. There was no hope. Bruce closed his eyes but could not escape in sleep; faces of dead men haunted him. 'Coward,' they accused, 'we died for your kingdom. Defeatist.'

In one corner of his cave a spider swung from a thin strand. An insignificant creature, it was attempting to attach itself to the smooth overhang opposite. Already it had tried a dozen times, but as Bruce watched, it launched itself in another futile swing. Legs stretching, the spider reached the wall, sleek with slime. It found no purchase and fell back defeated.

Bruce found himself intrigued by the tiny thing. He watched, fascinated, as it gathered its strength for another assault. It was like himself, struggling against the impossible, a minuscule creature attempting a gigantic task. If there was no hope for him, there was none for the spider.

The silken web caught hold; a tiny protuberance in the rock had escaped the slime and the spider had found enough hold. From here the spider expanded its web as Bruce watched. If a spider could achieve the impossible, could he give up so easily?

The accusation was gone from the faces of his dead followers as Bruce left the cave, to breathe the fresh Arran air. Scotland beckoned, a kingdom was to be won.

45

Fairy Legends

There is nothing exclusively Scottish about fairy legends: they are so widespread around the world as to be commonplace. Like other nations Scotland has good and bad fairies, helpful and destructive fairies. Their origins are disputed, their age uncer-tain, their truth unknown. Is there any truth at all in the legends? It is hard to tell, but one significant fact is the lack of stories concerning the gossamer-winged variety in Scotland, however much these seem to abound elsewhere. Most Scottish fairies are more practical and a lot less delicate than that.

One theory is that fairies are a folk memory of a people who lived in Scotland back in Neolithic times; a people so technologically backward that they did not use iron – hence the fairy fear of that metal – but so close to nature they were skilled with plants and animals, and so nervous they lived underground in fairy hills. These hills are scattered quite profusely round Scotland, each with a secret doorway and many with a legend attached. The Eildon Hills in the Borders were used by the fairies; Thomas the Rhymer gained his powers there. Tomnahurich in Inverness was equally famous and once held two pipers for centuries; they did not emerge until around 1930. And in the Highlands the name 'Shee' signifies fairy. Glen Shee, Schiehallion – landmarks of ancient occupation.

It is not necessary to travel far back in time to discover a similar situation. The bushmen (or Han) people of Southern Africa lived with Stone Age technology and were driven to the deserts by Bantu and Boer invasions. These bushmen were incredible trackers and hunters who lived as close to nature as man ever has. As close as the Aborigines of Australia, or the indigenous peoples of the New Guinea jungle – or the fairies of Alba?

Belief in the 'People of Peace', as they were known, died hard. Even with the Industrial Revolu-tion in full swing, superstition – or folk memory – remained strong in Scotland.

The Fairies of Lewis

One day in 1831 a crofter was walking along a Lewis beach; there had been a heavy storm the previous night so perhaps the man was gathering seaweed to manure his land. Instead of seaweed he found the remains of an ancient building whose centuries-old covering of sand had been dragged away by the sea.

Curious, the crofter prodded at the walls with his spade, dug around a little to see what he could find. He stopped, spade poised, when he realized there was a tiny man glowering at him, bearded face set above a kite-shaped shield, long sword ready in his right hand. Muttering, the crofter stepped back, his heel kicked at something else in the sand; he looked down and there was another little man, baleful eyes glaring. That was enough: throwing away his spade the crofter ran.

When the Lewisman gabbled his tale to his wife, she proved to be less susceptible to superstition. By laughter or jeers she forced her husband back to the ruins. It was an eerie place, the forlorn remains of a dwelling, the crash of the Atlantic, the still, staring figures. Hurriedly, averting his eyes, the crofter lifted the first of the fairies – for that is what he believed they were. The creature did not struggle, nor did the next, nor the next and soon the crofter had dozens of the little people safe in his bag.

More than likely it was his wife who encouraged the crofter to display and finally sell the strange figures. A local man bought all 78 ivory chessmen which had been buried since the Vikings ruled the islands. Now some are on display in the Museum of Antiquities in Edinburgh but copies are easily available – direct replicas of Viking chess pieces.

If the pieces had not been recognized, would there be another mysterious fairy tale from the islands?

That story, with its ready explanation, is an exception. Most of the Scottish fairies were not so easily run to earth. The descriptions vary with the fairy type but, overall, are surprisingly uniform: small people dressed in green – the Celtic mystic colour – who live in fairy hills. At night they dance and party, or steal children, replacing the unfortunate child with one of their own, a changeling. Sometimes humans were enticed inside the fairy dwellings (as at Inverness) and when they emerged they found time had passed much faster than they realized.

But not only hills were sacred to the fairies. In Skye there was a fairy bridge and, better known, a fairy flag.

The Fairy Flag

Turreted and majestic, the castle of Dunvegan presides over Dunvegan Loch in the north-west of Skye. The setting is from a fairy tale, with the sharp blue loch contrasting with green trees and austere stonework, distant hills and the plaintive cry of sea and shorebirds. As would be expected in such a stimulating island as Skye, Dunvegan Castle has a history long and dramatic.

Among its treasures are Rory Mor's Drinking Horn and the Dunvegan Cup, paintings by Raeburn and Ramsay and the great two-handed swords of warrior chiefs. However, above these, and central to the well-being of clan MacLeod who claim the castle as their heart, is the Fairy Flag.

With a name so evocative, it could come as a disappointment actually to view the flag. In appearance it is certainly not spectacular, being neither large nor particularly colourful. Originally yellow, the colour has faded to a mustard brown and at some time in its past the flag has been darned with red, the patches known as elf-spots. Not an inspiring sight, but the legend more than makes up for that; the history adds lustre to what is definitely an ancient banner.

Centuries ago one of the chiefs of MacLeod, possibly Malcolm the fat and good, or Ian his son, fell in love with a fairy. Such occurrences were not so uncommon then as they have become today. The two married and were very happy together until the fairy bore a son for the MacLeod. At once her own people called her back and, sadly, she had to go.

At Fairy Bridge, not far from Dunvegan and once frequently visited by the People of Peace, husband and wife parted for the last time. The farewell would be tearful, with the fairy mother clinging to her newborn son and the MacLeod reluctant to lose his fairy bride. However, there was no choice and in the end the couple parted.

That night Dunvegan was alive with noise as the clan celebrated the birth of an heir to the chief. Music and laughter, harping and dancing with wine and whisky flowing free. It sounded so hearty a gathering that the nursemaid who had been left with the baby deserted her charge to join in.

As babies will, young MacLeod kicked off his coverings and soon began to feel the cold. As he let the world know of his discomfort his bawls were unheeded amidst the raucous party noise, but far outside in the cool dark of the Hebridean night, a pair of ears heard the distress of her son.

Unseen, the fairy mother entered Dunvegan and came to her child. Covering him with a square of silk, she sang her son to sleep. In the meantime the nurse had returned, either out of a belated sense of duty or because she heard the singing, and when she entered the room she could see nobody except for the baby.

The singing continued, a lilting cradle song, but there was no singer. Naturally afraid, the nurse lifted the baby in his silken shawl, carried him to the chief and confessed what had happened. Simultaneously there was another voice in the room, telling MacLeod that if the clan was ever in danger he could wave the flag to save it. However, he was allowed only three waves and then the flag would be taken away by an unseen being – and the standard-bearer with it.

Clan MacLeod took the fairy message to be true. The flag was cased, MacCrimmachs chosen as the 12-man bodyguard for its protection and to date it has been waved twice in battle, both times successfully. Once, when the MacLeods were being defeated by MacDonalds – their mortal foes – the flag was waved and the MacLeod force seemed 10 times as large, shocking clan Donald. On another occasion – the battle of Glendale – Lady MacLeod and her maid were in danger but the cased flag was displayed and the MacLeods redoubled their efforts. Whether the clan was more afraid of losing the flag or the chief's wife is uncertain.

However, there are other stories to explain the origin of the flag. Specialists claim that the flag is

49

from the Orient and hazard that it might have been brought back from the crusades: there was a strong contingent of Orkney crusaders in the late 12th century and Skyemen might well have joined them.

Another theory is that the Dunvegan flag may be the identical banner used by Harald Hardrada at the battle of Stamford Bridge in 1066. Hardrada, it will be remembered, was the Norse warrior who attempted to invade Saxon England. Hardrada had been a soldier in the Byzantine army at a time when the Byzantine Empire stretched well into Asia Minor; perhaps the flag was booty from some Eastern war. And, with Norse power lasting in most of the Hebrides until 1263, it is possible that some ancestor of the MacLeods gained the flag after Stamford.

There are other tales of magical flags in the north. Ragnar Lodbrok had a raven banner woven by his daughter; this flag was rampant when he was victorious but drooped if he was defeated. The Earl of Orkney battled beneath this famous raven banner. And a mainland clan, the MacPhersons, retain a magic green banner in their museum at Newtonmore.

Whatever the truth, none of these flags seem to have had the continuing psychological importance of Dunvegan's Fairy Flag. As late as World War II, warriors of clan MacLeod carried photographs of the flag into battle. As we know, that war ended in victory for the MacLeods and their allies.

It must also be remembered that the fairy mother sang a unique song to her son. The Dunvegan cradle song is ancient, and its words are of a form of archaic Gaelic – perhaps the form used by the People of Peace.

The Minister of Aberfoyle

To many, Aberfoyle is a gateway to the Highlands, situated as it is at the edge of the Queen Elizabeth Forest Park and the bristled country of the Trossachs. This is as it should be, but to one man Aberfoyle was the gateway to Fairyland.

This man was Dr Robert Kirk. If Kirk had been an ordinary man, a herd or a hind or a craftsman, and he had taken an interest in fairy activities, the matter might have provided mild amusement or scorn and almost certainly would have been forgotten long since, but Doctor Kirk was not ordinary.

Well educated, Kirk was a minister and the son of a minister. The seventh son, which could be thought-provoking in itself, given the powers sometimes attributed to seventh-born sons. And it was not as if Kirk was an outsider suddenly thrust into an alien environment, with his emotions destabilized to make him susceptible to any unusual event. Kirk had been born at Aberfoyle.

At the age of 20 and already a doctor of divinity, Kirk became minister of Balquhidder parish, a position he held for 21 years. This would be no light task in the turbulent 1660s, with clan Gregor roaming the glens and Campbell power expanding. During this time Kirk married twice and translated the Irish Bible into Scots Gaelic – a tremendous task. In 1685, at the age of 41 (too old to be a youth, too young to be senile and too steady to be eccentric), Kirk was transferred to the parish of Aberfoyle, a few miles to the south.

Overlooking the manse at Aberfoyle is Doon Hill which the locals were a little wary of. This hill was a 'Dun Sithean', they claimed: a fairy hill. Doon Hill fascinated the minister and in the evenings he would cross the fields and lie on the wooded slopes, listening to sounds he claimed to hear coming from inside the hill. It must have been trying for his wife, searching for him night after night on the eerie flanks of the fairy hill.

Five years after taking over the parish, Kirk began to write a work entitled 'The Secret Commonwealth of Elves, Fawns and Fairies'. This unusual composition explained why Kirk had been acting so peculiarly; he had been communicating with a fairyland inside Doon Hill.

Kirk termed the fairies Doine Shi (People of Peace) and said they had 'apparel and speech like that of the people and country under which they live'. So much for the pointed hat and curly-toed slippers of storybook elves. 'They speak little, and that by way of whistling . . . Their bodies be so plyable through the subillity of the Spirits that agitate them, that they can make them appear or disappear att pleasure.'

Kirk described the life of the fairies and their gift of second sight. He gave an instance of their fear of cold iron and of their ability to transport people from place to place – an ability highlighted in other Scottish fairy myths. Perhaps Kirk had been experiencing hallucinations but if so his account was remarkably lucid, and by writing it down he could not possibly benefit himself. There could be no trickery involved; Robert Kirk genuinely believed that what he wrote was factual.

Whatever the reasons, Kirk had little chance to explain his writings. One May night in 1692 Kirk left the manse for the last time. As usual, his destination was Doon Hill but this time when his patient wife found him he was dead, lying on the hillside in his nightshirt. Apparently the minister had collapsed in a fit.

Now begins the greatest mystery of this man. Even as his coffin was lowered into its grave in Aberfoyle Churchyard, men muttered that Kirk was not inside: the coffin was filled with rocks.

Dead or not, Kirk – or something in his form – came to one of his relations with the startling information that he was trapped inside Fairyland and would only materialize when his child was baptized. Kirk told his relative to warn Graham of Duchray, a cousin who was to be at the baptism, that when Kirk appeared Duchray was to throw a knife over his head. This would enable the minister to come back into the world.

As Kirk's relation hesitated to speak to Duchray about his deceased visitor – naturally enough given the climate of the times – Kirk came back a second time and persuaded him with the threat of nightly visitations. The man spoke to Duchray.

The day of the baptism came and Duchray brought his iron knife, but when Kirk appeared, apparently as healthy as ever, Duchray was too astounded to do more than stare. With a censorious look on his face, Kirk walked past, out another door and disappeared. He was never seen again.

So what is the truth? Were Kirk's fairies supernatural beings? Or creatures from another dimension? Or is this just another Scottish legend which has become twisted with the passage of time?

Scottish Monsters

Discuss monsters in Scotland and the chances are that Loch Ness will enter the conversation. There has been so much attention paid to the famous Loch Ness monster or 'Nessie' that it is a subject hard to avoid, yet to concentrate solely on her is to perform an injustice to the many other monsters which reside, or have resided, within Scotland.

Over the past few decades there have been sightings of unexplained things at Loch Morar and on the flanks of Ben Macdhui. Loch Morar is said to have a monster named Morag and there have been suggestions that an underground passage connects Loch Morar to Loch Ness along which Morag (or Nessie) swims. It is one theory among many.

The monster which has its home on Ben Macdhui appears more related to Bigfoot or the Yeti than to Nessie. 'The Big Grey Man' of Ben Macdhui roams the slopes of the 4296-feet-high mountain. Described as a grey, man-shaped creature 10 feet tall and sometimes – incongruously – wearing a black 'lum' (or top) hat, this creature tends to haunt a cairn on the slope and has been known to follow, or chase, walkers as far as Braemar. This is 11 miles from Ben Macdhui.

With the steadily increasing popularity of hill-walking and mountaineering, this Grey Man has been glimpsed more often of late but it remains as elusive and tantalizing as its cousin in the Himalayas. Schiehallion too, the fairy hill of the Caledonians, has a monster in the shape of a dog-like beast which appears from nowhere and follows walkers.

The Linton Worm

However, not all Scottish monsters have been as shy as Morag and the Grey Man. Once there were dragons in Scotland, although they were often given the more prosaic term of 'worm'. At the village of Dalry in the Glenkens there was a worm which lived round a hillock named the Mote until the local blacksmith disposed of it.

Farther north, at the Kirkton of Strathmartine in Angus, it was a local lad named Martin who acted as dragon-killer, but better known than either of these was the Linton Worm.

This dragon lived in the worm's glen, in a long tunnel bored into Linton Hill, near the English border. Twelve feet long and as thick as a man, the worm was marked like an adder and slithered from its hole twice a day – at dawn and dusk to eat. The hunger of the Linton Worm had emptied the locality, for even the boldest hunter had been unable to harm it; arrows and spears alike were useless against the worm's armoured scales, livestock just vanished into the poisonous, fanged jaws.

A local laird, John Somerville, had been in England until he heard of this monster. Curious, he crossed the Cheviots and watched the worm in action. Somerville noted certain things which were interesting. First, the worm could not slither backwards; it had to move in a circle to get back into its den. Second, when it saw anything too large to eat, it stopped, mouth wide open.

Withdrawing from the area, Somerville prepared to kill the beast. As had been frequently proved, an ordinary spear was useless, so Somerville made one twice the normal length and sheathed most of the shaft with iron to protect it from the worm's fiery breath. As the spear point would not be strong enough to pierce the scales, Somerville made an attachment whereby a burning peat could be carried. With this as a weapon, and his horse trained to accept the reek of peat smoke, Somerville set out. He rode alone; the Borderers refused to help him, although they gathered to watch.

Dawn on the chosen day and John Somerville waited at the den of the worm. As the ugly head appeared at the entrance, he lit the peat, placed it on the attachment on his lance point and spurred his horse to advance. At the sight of man and horse, far too big to eat, the worm opened its mouth in astonishment and Somerville lunged forward with his lance.

Through the poisonous jaws and on, down the cavernous throat, the iron-bound lance thrust the smouldering peat deep inside the worm's vitals. The shock of contact was terrible, nearly unhorsing Somerville, twisting the lance so it snapped. Agonized, the worm lashed and writhed; unable to slide back down the hole, its tail slashed at the tunnel roof until the earth collapsed, crushing the wounded beast beneath an avalanche of its own making.

Only when they were certain the worm was dead did the local people dig it out. When the king heard, he awarded land to John Somerville, and the event was commemorated by a carved stone which can still be seen at Linton Kirk.

The Loch Ness Monster

Returning to Iona from his mission to Christianize the Picts, Saint Columba approached one of the crossing points of the River Ness. There was a small settlement here, and a group of people were digging a grave for a newly dead man. When Columba asked how the man had died he was told he had been killed by a monster who lived in the loch.

This interested the saint but did not seem to worry him, for he let one of his monks, Lugne Mocumin, swim across the Ness to fetch a boat which bobbed against the opposite bank. Celtic monks were a hardy breed and Lugne cheerfully leaped into the water and began to swim to the boat. He was about halfway across when the monster reappeared.

Columba, however, was equal to any monster. 'The blessed man raised his holy hand,' Adamnan, his biographer, wrote, 'while all the rest were stupified with terror, and commanded the monster, saying: "Thou shalt go no further nor touch the man. Go back with all speed!"' As extra insurance, the saint made the sign of the cross. That was enough for the monster: it fled.

It is nearly 60 years since the spate of recent sightings began, or at least since the monster became popular in the public imagination. Perhaps the advent of tourism has something to do with it, the relative ease of travel in the Highlands, or the increased use of media coverage so that what was once of purely local importance has become widely known.

If there seems a lot of fuss generated about the possible existence of an unidentified animal in an otherwise obscure Scottish loch, maybe it is an expression of modern escapism. Perhaps it is better to concentrate on something interesting, unimportant and romantic than on the relentless realities of the world.

It was in spring 1933 that a local couple saw something like a whale on the waters of Loch Ness. The *Inverness Courier* reported a 'Strange Spectacle on Loch Ness' and from there on Nessie has never looked back. That same year the term 'Loch Ness Monster' was used, and so the legend was born, or reborn, as the case may be. Every year now, people gather at the lochside, hoping for a glimpse of the supposed monster. Some are lucky, most are not.

At 24 miles long and about one mile wide, Loch Ness has not a huge area of surface water in which to hide a monster, less so a family of monsters. However the loch is deep: about 700 feet on average and far deeper in places; in fact, the loch is so deep it has never been known to freeze. At its widest and deepest point, where the ruined medieval Urquhart Castle presides over the dark water, Nessie most often surfaces. Here the mountains subside and Glen Urquhart gouges deep into the land, a natural lay-by for Nessie. There is a dramatic photograph of something on the loch around here, with the shattered keep of Urquhart providing both scale and evidence of place. A tree branch perhaps? Or the wake of a boat? Perhaps – and perhaps not.

56

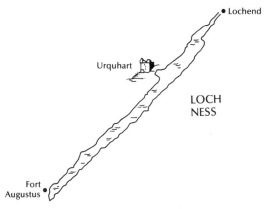

Not only simple cameras have been used to record the presence of something unusual in the loch. Many types of electronic gadgetry have been used, including sonar, radar scanning and mini-submarines, but all the results seem to have been inconclusive. Vague shapes, formless shadows in the murky waters, the detection of what could be a shoal of fish – or something else.

Then, in 1975, came a breakthrough. One of the many research parties from the United States claimed to have photographed a plesiosaur in the loch. Not only one, but an entire family, according to Sir Peter Scott of the World Wildlife Trust, could live in Loch Ness. This created pandemonium in the intellectual world and a debate on Nessie was to be held in Edinburgh.

This was the high point. The meeting was cancelled, the photographs were never published and the discussion reached the House of Commons. Was Nessie being protected? A reply was given when some members of parliament were allowed to study the evidence and, ultimately, Nessie was granted a Latin name, *Nessiteras Rhombopteryx*. This, apparently, means 'Loch Ness marvel with a diamond-shaped fin'. Anagrammatically, it also reads 'Monster hoax by Sir Peter S'.

Monster hoax? There have been something like 10 000 sightings since Columba's time; the beast has been seen on land and water, it has been chased by motorcyclists and has crossed the road in front of

motorcars; it has been photographed and traced on
sonar. It has been scoffed at by millions. Nessie is
part of the legend of Scotland and far too interesting
to dismiss as a mere hoax.

Kelpies, Mermaids and Other Beasts

Nations other than Scotland have their monsters,
their dragons, their beasts which haunt ragged
moorland and dense forests, but few can boast so
many, or such a variety. For Scotland is – or was –
frequented by kelpies, waterhorses, waterbulls,
mermaids, sealmen and the sinister Blue Men of the
Minch. The fact that a great number of these
legendary creatures comes from the Highlands
could be significant – is the Norse–Gaelic mind more
prone to contact with these entities? Or are they
merely more imaginative? Was the entire country
once rife with monster tales, but only in the less-
easy-to-tame landscape of the Highlands have they
been preserved?

One type of beast which has had no good said of it
is the kelpie or waterhorse. The kelpie often
appeared in the form of a horse which lured the
unwary rider to it. Once mounted it would gallop off
with its rider into the nearest river to certain death
by drowning.

At one harvest time by the Conon river, north of
Inverness, some men were plying their sickles on
the oats when they heard a deep voice: 'The hour
[of noon] is come but not the man.' They looked
round and there was a kelpie in the ford which lay in
the shadow of the church.

As the clock struck the fatal hour of noon a young
man appeared, riding towards the ford. Four of the
reapers stopped him, warned him of the kelpie's
words, but he ignored them and spurred on. Or he
tried to, for the reapers grabbed him, hauled him
from his horse and carried him into the church.
Locking the door, the reapers kept him there for an
hour before re-entering the church to set him free.

They were too late. As they were waiting outside,
the young man drowned in an ancient stone trough
within the church itself.

Often the waterhorse disguised himself as a handsome young man and wooed a local lass to her death

in the dark waters of a loch. On one occasion in Badenoch the tables were turned as the horse came ashore as a lovely girl and only gave herself away when she laughed with a loud neigh. In this case her lover had the presence of mind to draw a dirk and stab his companion. As she died the girl changed back into the slimed creature from the loch.

Given her immense seaboard, it is not surprising that there are a number of mermaid tales from Scotland. What is surprising is how recent some of them are. As late as 1947 a fisherman from Muck met a mermaid combing her hair, while Sandwood Bay in north-west Sutherland was a well-known haunt of the creatures in the early years of this century. A legend tells of a hoard of jewels deep beneath the sea off Duncansby Head, which was looked after by a beautiful mermaid. It was a lonely life for the mermaid, but the sea god felt sorry for her and allowed her to have as many companions as she could keep. Now she has scores of once human lovers for ever bound to the sea bed with chains of fine gold.

Or there was the poignant little tale from Iona, where the mermaid felt in love with a saint. The saint was unable to return her devotion as the mermaid's soul was not human. In the cool morning and the wide Hebridean night, the mermaid swam ashore to pray for a soul, but always the sea called her back. She was a sad mermaid, and cried bitterly; her tears landed on the blessed shore and were miraculously solidified into the pebbles which are there today.

Not so pleasant are the Blue Men of the Minch. These, also known as 'storm kelpies', frequent the Shiant (charmed) islands to the east of Lewis. In the sound between the islands, the Sruth nam feae Gorma (Stream of the Blue Men), they float among the choppy waves, blue men with faces half-hidden by grey beards. When a boat approaches they ask the Master Mariner riddles, to which he must reply correctly or be dragged beneath the waves to the Blue Men's subterranean caves.

There may be an undercurrent of fact in this story, for the Norsemen, who dominated the area for so long, were known to use slaves taken from North African vessels. These unfortunate Berbers wore blue, veiled clothes, not unlike the infamous

Toureg, known as the 'blue men of the desert', who originate from the mountainous interior of Algeria.

Climatic changes in the 17th century resulted in the cold currents of the Arctic shifting further south, and that could account for the arrival of Eskimoes and some of the sealmen legends. Possibly this same phenomenon explains the tales of the silkies, or selkies. These seal-like creatures had the ability to come on to land whenever there was a full moon. Once on land the silkies discarded their seal skin and danced happily, but in this condition they were very vulnerable to human depravations. There is a story from the Northern Isles of three brothers who stole the skins of three of these silkies. The elder brothers kept their prey as wives until they died, heart-broken at being unable to return to the sea, but the youngest brother returned the seal skin to his silkie captive and she then took him to her home under the waves. There they lived happily as man and wife.

Interestingly, as late as the last century – and possibly after that – fishermen of the north-east coast who had webbed feet were said to be 'luckentaed' and could not be drowned. Webbed feet were supposed to be a sign of the silkie in human form.

Scottish Freebooters

Pirates, outlaws, reivers and others who live on and beyond the fringes of the law have a fascination for us all. Perhaps it is because the vast majority of us are constrained by a network of rules and regulations which keep us firmly in our place. There are few wild places to escape to, except in the fringes of the mind, or in the memory of days where opportunities for escape were greater, or in retrospect, appear greater. Maybe this too is a myth, a folk memory of the thousands of years when people were hunter-gatherers free to wander where they willed – or again, it could merely be a subconscious desire to put one over on those who would rule us.

It is a complex question which has been simplified throughout Scotland's past by many individuals. Once again, however, Scotland seems to have produced a colourful collection of these freebooters. One reason for this could be the clash of two opposing cultures, Gaelic and Teutonic, of which the Teutonic was materially and numerically stronger and appeared to dominate for long periods. However, the Gaelic culture was to survive, and now it seems that the Teutonic culture, which for so long threatened the Gael, is itself under attack.

As the Gaelic folk heroes were in part created to expunge the bitterness of defeat, the legends of fearless Borderers and daring gypsies were spoken by a people always in the shadow of the gallows' noose. Is that not true of most folk heroes, Robin Hood, Jesse James, Ned Kelly? The underdog is normally the hero, but often only when it is safe to make him so; for how many of us would like to have met Rob Roy going about his business, or Johnnie Armstrong face to face?

Rob Roy MacGregor

Arguably, there is no one by the name of MacGregor

as famous as Rob Roy MacGregor (1671–1734), the notorious Scottish freebooter. Rob himself would have had no argument with this, for he was never one to hide the light of his countenance under a bushel. And the clan itself, the Griogair, 'the Children of the Mist', would think it only proper that their name should survive and be exalted while that of their most relentless persecutor, clan Campbell, should be for ever linked – however unfairly – with the massacre of Glencoe.

Roy Roy has been likened to a Scottish Robin Hood, an outlaw who braved the redcoats, laughed at authority and made Glengyle a Sherwood Forest where only his own people felt secure. The reality is grander, for the MacGregors were more than mere outlaws. *Is Rioghaid mo Dhream*, they claim, 'Royal is my Race', and boast descent from Griogair, son of Alpin, King of Scots in the early ninth century. Malcolm, chief of the clan, fought at Bruce's side at Bannockburn and followed Edward Bruce on his Irish adventure, retiring wounded from the fatal encounter at Dundalk. The rise of the Campbells, who also supported Bruce, meant lean times for MacGregor, although the clan endured for centuries.

With Campbell prodding, the Crown ordered letters of 'fire and sword' – legal murder and pillage – against the MacGregors, and the Colquhouns of Luss helped in these raids. This led to MacGregor retaliation and the battle of Glen Fruin in 1603. Over a hundred Colquhouns were slain, but so were some luckless Lowlanders who had come to watch the fun. It is difficult to feel sympathy for them, for they left the security of their homes in the expectation of witnessing others being slaughtered, only to become victims themselves.

The outcome, however, was equally grim for the MacGregors; by an act of the Privy Council, dated 3 April 1603, the very name of MacGregor was proscribed; all who had taken part in the battle were prohibited from carrying any weapon other than a knife with its point broken or rounded off and could not meet in groups of more than four. The penalty for breaking any of these rules was death.

Amongst themselves the MacGregors, no doubt, used their own names. To sign documents, or appear to the world outside their own clan, they used the names of neighbouring peoples. Campbell, Graham, Drummond, Stewart. The clan remained united; some hundreds fought for King Charles I under Patrick MacGregor of Glenstrae. In gratitude, Charles II annulled the statutes of 1633 against them in 1661, but William of Orange reinstated them in 1693. It was in this new era of persecution that Rob Roy came into prominence.

His mother a Campbell, his father Lieutenant-Colonel MacGregor of Glengyle, Rob Roy was the second son so was never chief of the clan, although he was its captain in time of war. Rob Roy was born around 1671 in Glengyle, and seemed to be fairly law-abiding in his youth – for a MacGregor – although this could be disputed. There is a story about the village of Kippen when Rob Roy was supposedly a lawful cattle-drover. This would be around 1691, when William would have just been made king.

Rob Roy was droving 200 cattle to the tryst (market) at Buchlyvie, crossing the fords of Frew on the way. How he came by the cattle is arguable, but perhaps he was working honestly for his living at the time. When he came to Kippen all that changed, for the temptation of the villagers' cattle was difficult for any Highlander, brought up on tales of reiving and raiding, to resist. Rob Roy swept through the place, driving everything movable before him.

At the fords of Frew, one of the few places where the huge Flanders Moss was passable, Rob Roy was caught by a party of dragoons from Cardross but he used the land and his MacGregors to panic them. What the good folk of Kippen thought of all this romantic thievery is not mentioned in the legend. No doubt they laughed heartily at the antics of that jolly outlaw, Rob Roy, as they looked at a bleak and hungry future.

Shortly after, Rob Roy married Mary MacGregor of Cromar, his second cousin and a match for him in every way. Perhaps it was the responsibilities of marriage which quietened the wild streak in him, for he seems to have returned to droving for some years, borrowing money from the Duke of Montrose to keep himself solvent. In this he made a mistake, for it was a major cause of subsequent events; this, the fact he was a Jacobite in an extremely disturbed Scotland, and the proud MacGregor blood which flowed through him.

When Rob Roy discovered he was bankrupt in 1712, he slipped into the hills until the matter passed over. Montrose sent Graham of Killearn, his factor, with a body of men to Rob Roy's house in Inversnaid at the head of Loch Katrine (loch of the caterans, or thieves). Rob Roy was not there, but his lands were seized, his houses plundered and his wife and children evicted in midwinter. To any man this would lead to anger, but there would be little they could do. Rob Roy MacGregor was not just any man and his wife was as implacable as he.

From that day, Rob Roy and his clansmen waged an open war of attrition on the Duke of Montrose and Graham of Killearn, his factor. The duke's estates spread to the Highland border, temptingly easy to raid, and Rob Roy vowed they would keep him and his in cattle until his last day. He kept his word. The raids began, and so did the legends.

Graham of Killearn was Rob Roy's principal target; once, Rob Roy found him at the inn at Chapel-darroch (then a township, now shrunk to a farm) and quietly kidnapped him. The factor was taken to the shores of Loch Katrine, thrown on a boat and rowed to Eilean Dubh at the head of the loch. Here Killearn was held until Rob decided to let him go unharmed; for Rob Roy was no killer.

On another occasion, the factor was collecting rents at the same inn when Rob Roy looked through a window and observed him. Killearn was placing a bag of money in a cupboard, claiming he would give it all away for Rob Roy's head. At this time Rob Roy had only one man with him, but he shouted commands to a score of imaginary followers and boldly entered the inn with his sole companion. After forcing Killearn to write a receipt to each tenant, Rob Roy used the factor's money to buy food and drink for all the company, warned Killearn to sit still for an hour and left the inn.

Rob Roy, however, was more than just a taunter of Killearn. He was a blackmailer, of the original kind where blackmail meant payment to prevent cattle being taken, and any man of property or wealth could be a victim. (Blackmail was a protection racket which originated in the Borders in the Middle Ages.) The Campbells suffered: Sir Colin Campbell of Aberwehill and Kilbryde was blackmailed, although his son, James, was bold enough to refuse payment. Perhaps his father being Lord Justice Clerk had an effect on him. Rob Roy waited until James was at dinner with a gathering of friends, rounded up the Kilbryde cattle and demanded payment or he would take the lot. The shamefaced laird had no option but to pay up.

In the middle of his career, Rob Roy had a diversion as the Jacobite rising of 1715 erupted. Captain of the clan, Rob Roy led his followers to the battle at Sheriffmuir, arrived late and halted at the Allan Water. Here he stayed, his MacGregors a disciplined guard as the Highlanders of the left wing withdrew from Argyll's redcoats. Not a heroic part, but the battle was already lost and his first responsibility was to his clan, not to a man who might be king.

There were other brushes with the redcoats. For instance, the time when the Glasgow volunteers marched north to claim a 1000-pound reward Rob Roy had on his head – and fled at first sight of the MacGregors. There was the near-forgotten rising of 1719 and the battle in Glenshiel where 300 Spaniards surrendered. There was the encounter at Duchray Castle when Rob Roy slipped out the back door while the Graham sisters kept dragoon officers amused at the front.

There was also the fort built at Inversnaid. Traces

of this building still remain on a hillock overlooking the Snaid and Arklet Water, but it had a very difficult task. Twice before it was built, Rob Roy destroyed it, and the redcoats stationed here, with wild MacGregors watching their movements, must never have let their hands stray from their muskets.

That fort was the only one built in the Highlands in this period; together with the roads designed by Wade it was intended to quell the Highlanders, of whom Wade had said, 'and the MacGregors on the borders of Argyllshire. They go out in parties from 10 to 30 men, traverse large tracts of mountains until they arrive at the Lowlands . . . they drive the stolen cattle in the night time and in the day remain in the tops of the mountains or in the woods, with which the Highlands abound, and take the first occasion to sell them at the fairs and markets that are annually held.'

It could have been a job description for Rob Roy himself. A man of less than average height, solidly built and nimble of mind, Rob Roy's spectre haunts the hills and Lowlands from Balquhidder to Kippen and beyond. It is pleasing to remember that he died in his bed, his wife Mary at his side, and on the land he claimed as his own.

Johnnie Armstrong

What the MacGregors were to the south-west Highlands, the Armstrongs were to the south-west Borders, and what Rob Roy was to the MacGregors, Johnnie Armstrong (d.1530) has become to the Armstrongs. Outside the imaginings of mythology, however, there was very little similarity between the two.

It must be remembered that the clan system operated in the Borders as well as the Highlands, although the organization was not identical. There was no Gaelic culture, nothing like the same sense of remoteness from the rest of Scotland and no history of political independence. The Borders were right in the forefront of any invasion route and therefore, to a large extent, in the mainstream of Scottish military and political history.

This meant that while a raid by, for example, a MacDonald or a MacNab could be tolerated to a degree, a similar incursion by Border Armstrongs or

Kerrs, because of the close proximity of England and the possibility of war, could not. There was another side to the coin; the Borderer could always slip across the frontier and claim protection from the neighbouring country.

In his moment of crisis, Johnnie Armstrong of Gilnockie ('Black Jock' to his contemporaries) did not; he was not given the opportunity.

> On the border were the Armstrongs, able men,
> Somewhat unruly, and very ill to tame.

As the old rhyme says, Johnnie's clan lived on the border. They were based in Liddesdale, a narrow stark valley hard by the border, or on the Debateable Land (between Esk and Sark), an area of perhaps 50 square miles, claimed by Scotland and England and left empty, by agreement, by both. It was illegal to build or live on this land and only the worst characters, the most murderous outlaws and the hardest riders stayed here. Johnnie Armstrong's tower of Gilnockie was here, on the bank of the Esk.

It is easy to underestimate the fighting strength of these southern clans, but Johnnie's Armstrongs could raise around 3000 men, mounted on hobblers (sturdy Border ponies) and armed with sword and lance. They were a formidable force and Johnnie, with his brother Thomas, Laird of Mangerton, Sim the Laird of Whitehaugh and Ill Will Armstrong used them effectively. Johnnie raided a wide area, mainly – he would later claim exclusively – into England. Blackmail, extortion, cattle-reiving, murder, Johnnie was a chief exponent of them all.

In 1527 Johnnie participated in, or perhaps led, a raid to Newcastle to free some English Lisles. It could have been this deep raid which angered Lord Dacre, the English warden, into leading a force to drive the Armstrongs from the Debateable Land.

Although the idea was excellent, so was the Armstrongs' intelligence service. They heard about Lord Dacre's advance, waited for him and sent him home with his tail between his legs. Dacre came a second time and used cannon to destroy Johnnie's tower, but Johnnie could easily build another. During this time he was in England, systematically stripping Netherby, a village near Carlisle, of anything worth having, and destroying a mill of Dacre's out of spite.

In 1529 Armstrongs and English wardens clashed again when the warden's men, led by a Nicholas Ridley, followed an Armstrong raid into Liddesdale and left a score of prisoners in Armstrong hands. Young King James V gathered his council together and decided on a judicial raid to quell finally the Armstrong power. It was high time.

A number of ballads deal with the king's meeting with Johnnie Armstrong. The king proffered some form of safe conduct, with at least the offer of a partial pardon to all Armstrongs who submitted to him, and Johnnie accepted the royal words in good faith. At Caerlanrig in Upper Teviotdale the two parties met, Johnnie with two score or so of his men riding tall behind him, King James with his nucleus of royal troops backed by local riders, some of whom doubtless had a feud with the Armstrongs.

Close to, the king realized what sort of man Johnnie Armstrong was. Instead of a ragged outlaw begging for his life, here was the leader of a disciplined body of men, richly clothed and armed as well as any royal soldiers. 'What,' said the king, 'wants yon knave that a king should have?' Nothing, except royalty itself, apparently, but James had more men handy and they held Johnnie, Thomas and more than 30 others.

Johnnie, however, was a Borderer, ever ready to wriggle and plead his way out of a tight situation. He offered himself and 40 men to the king as a royal hit force; he promised that he had never robbed in Scotland and asked James to name him any Englishmen, of any rank up to a duke, and he would bring him back to Scotland, dead or alive. There was little, if any, exaggeration in these claims; Black Jock could do what he promised, but James ignored the blandishments and gave his pronouncement: a hempen noose and a nearby tree.

'It is folly to seek grace at a graceless face.' Johnnie retained his pride as he bit back, 'Had I known this, I should have lived on the Borders in despite of King Harry [Henry VIII] and you both.' King Harry, he pointed out, would 'downweigh my best horse with gold, to know that I were condemned to die this day'.

King James V met Johnnie on 5 July 1530. Before the eighth day of the month, Johnnie was dead.

The Armstrongs continued to ride.

James MacPherson

James MacPherson (d.1700) is one of the lesser-known Scottish freebooters, which does not mean he is one of the least interesting. Reivers (robbers), outlaws, pirates and the like thrive on the borders where two nations or two cultures meet, and James MacPherson was no exception. He operated in the north-east Lowlands of Buchan and Moray, with the great granite mass of the Grampians as a backdrop. Added to this, MacPherson had gypsy blood, for he was the illegitimate son of a laird and a young gypsy girl.

Either by choice or through lack of it, James became a member of the gypsy clan and took to a life of robbery. At this time there was a little more prosperity in the Scottish Lowlands, lairds were building homes which were more like mansions and less like castles, markets were more common with the gradual demise of clan and national war.

This wealth did not naturally filter down to the poor, so James lent nature a hand. With his gypsy band at his back, James MacPherson roamed the broad Lowlands, terrorizing the rich and aiding the poor. He was a carefree, cheerful outlaw, for he was as renowned for his musical skills as much as his criminal ones and his prowess on the fiddle was spoken of with admiration.

Like most outlaws, however, James made enemies among the lairds, notably one Duff of Braco, and Duff gathered a force to capture the musical free-booter. In this period there were many fairs in the country, the only days off people had, and an excuse for jollity. To judge by the ballads of such events, the fairs were raucous places, with all sorts of illicit and immoral goings-on; a natural magnet for James MacPherson.

The Laird of Braco knew this well.

As James moved through the crowd at Banff fair he was followed by Braco's men. Possibly he saw them, perhaps he turned to fight, but a woman, perhaps a jealous lover or just public-spirited, played a decisive part in his capture. Leaning from an upstairs window, she dropped a blanket over the outlaw's head, which smothered him, deprived him of sight and restricted his movements. Like this, James was an easy victim for Braco's men.

A trial followed, with the inevitable sentence of death by hanging. James MacPherson was tossed into a dungeon to await his last day but instead of planning his escape, James turned to his music for solace. The rant he composed, 'MacPherson's Farewell', is still sung and some of the lines are memorable, although the master touch of Burns has since helped:

> O what is death but parting breath?
> On many a bloody plain
> I've dared his face, and in this place
> I scorn him yet again!

There is a jauntiness here, a scornful jest in spite of Braco and his hempen noose, but bitterness in the line 'I die by treacherie.'

As James was led to the rope, he did not know there was a reprieve coming. Even if he had, he might not have acted differently. Musician to the last, James played the tune he had composed, sang the taunting, biting words and then offered his fiddle to any of his gypsy brethren who wanted it. None came forward – perhaps they feared being caught by Braco – so James hefted the violin by its neck, splintered it over the head of the executioner and, as Banff's clock struck the hour, jumped from the fatal ladder, rope round his neck.

Only Braco knew about the reprieve, only Braco knew that the clock had been put forward a quarter of an hour to ensure that James was hanged.

Ironically, Braco is remembered only for his deviousness while MacPherson the outlaw is recalled by the song he wrote. MacPherson won the test of legend, but that same legend has glossed romance over the facts.

James MacPherson, under some form of protection from the Laird of Grant, led 30 so-called 'gypsies' at the end of the 17th century. These gypsies were more likely to be sorners (violent beggars who sometimes banded together to attack cottages and hamlets) and they swaggered into the market towns of Elgin, Forres and Banff to the notes of a piper. They marched armed with basket-hilted broadswords, dirks and matchlock muskets, but did not immediately attack their victims. Instead they watched, noting who sold most cattle and pocketed most money. These were MacPherson's chosen victims.

Perhaps MacPherson's attachment to the Laird of Grant gave rise to the story of his illegitimate birth – or perhaps Grant was indeed helping his natural son. Either way, MacPherson's career was long but eventually ended on the gallows. There is a lot of truth in the legend, but also notable gaps.

But perhaps this is the purpose of a legend, to distill the essence of truth, add to it the nobler qualities of humanity and remove the sordid aspects. To make an uplifting story which will be remembered long after the man or woman it commemorates has passed away. If so, may the legend-makers remain.

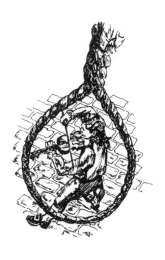